# WRITTEN BY ADAM BRAY

# CONTENTS

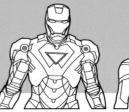

# LET'S BEGIN AT THE BEGINNING...

*Overwhelmed by the Marvel movies? Confused by which Super Hero is which, or mixed up between films? Complete beginner or just feeling a bit rusty? Well, you're in luck!*

## 1. YOU ARE NOT ALONE

Fear not, for not everyone has seen all the Marvel movies. Whether you have or haven't, this is the book for you!

## 2. START WITH THE BASICS

The Basics section gives the general lowdown on all things Marvel movie-related. Start here, so you don't feel lost!

## 3. MOVIE BY MOVIE

Work your way through the films. We've made it easy, giving you a quick overview of each one.

## 4. LEARN MORE

Burning questions? Delve deeper into each movie's Q&As and get the lowdown you need on who, what, where, when, and why.

## 5. READY TO ROLL

You'll know your Lokis from your Laufeys in no time, and be ready to dazzle others with your newfound knowledge!

"This doesn't have to get any messier."

NICK FURY

# MARVEL CINEMATIC UNIVERSE: THE BASICS

WHO, WHAT, WHERE, WHEN, WHY...

OK, so my first question is...

# WHAT IS MARVEL?

*I know there are lots of Super Hero movies out there and they're really popular. What's so marvellous about it all? Where did it all begin?*

## WHAT IS MARVEL?

Marvel is a lot of things. It started as a comic book company, with roots going all the way back to 1939. Since then, Marvel has created many different properties based on its comic books and lengthy roster of super-powered characters. These have included the MCU movies, live-action TV shows, cartoons, video games, and toys. In 2009, Marvel became part of the Walt Disney Company.

Phase One

## BUT WHAT DOES "MCU" STAND FOR?

MCU stands for "Marvel Cinematic Universe." The MCU is an ongoing series of awesome movies that follow the adventures of Marvel characters. All MCU movies are interconnected to varying degrees. They are divided into Phases.

Phase Two

## WHAT IS A "PHASE?"

In the MCU, a Phase is a group of films that chart various story arcs. There have been three Phases so far. Phase One culminates with the Battle of New York in *Marvel's The Avengers* and Phase Two draws to a close in *Ant-Man*. Phase Three's latest movie is the Super Hero extravaganza, *Marvel Studios' Avengers: Infinity War*.

Phase Three

# ARE THE FILMS AND COMICS DIFFERENT?

Yes! The films take inspiration from the comics, but they are not adapted from them. Much has been changed—some of the comics were made a long time ago, so stories have been modernized and set in the present. Some storylines have been given to different characters, and some characters look very different from their illustrated versions.

# WHO CREATED THE COMICS?

Joe Simon and Jack Kirby created *Captain America* in 1941 (before the company came to be known as Marvel). Writer-editor Stan Lee and artist Jack Kirby created *The Avengers*, with the first issue debuting in 1963. The original comic book Avengers team consisted of Ant-Man, Wasp, Iron Man, Hulk, and Thor. Captain America joined in issue #4.

# SO WHO MAKES THE MCU MOVIES?

The MCU movies are created by Marvel Studios, which is a subsidiary of Walt Disney Studios. Several new Marvel films continue to be produced every year, so it's likely that as you read this, Marvel Studios are busy producing the next one for you. You lucky thing!

# A FEW CREATORS TO KNOW...

**Kevin Feige** is the president of Marvel Studios and a producer on all MCU films.

**Stan Lee** is the former editor-in-chief, publisher, and chairman of Marvel Comics (currently the chairman emeritus and a member of the editorial board). He has a cameo in every MCU film.

**Anthony and Joe Russo** (known as the Russo brothers) are the directors of *Captain America: The Winter Soldier*, *Captain America: Civil War*, and *Marvel Studios' Avengers: Infinity War*.

**James Gunn** is the director of the *Guardians of the Galaxy* films.

**Jon Favreau** is the director of the first two *Iron Man* films and plays recurring character, Harold "Happy" Hogan.

**Joss Whedon** is the director and a writer for *Marvel's The Avengers* (titled *Avengers Assemble* in the UK) and *Avengers: Age of Ultron*.

Jon Favreau (left) on the set of *Iron Man 2*, in character as Happy Hogan.

*I get it. There are a lot of these MCU movies, so...*

# WHO ARE THE MAIN PLAYERS?

**GROOT**
He is Groot!

*There's a big green guy, a man with a hammer, a woman named after a spider, a wizard, a tree, and a raccoon... what's the common thread? They all seem to be Super Heroes, right?*

## WHAT IS A SUPER HERO?

A Super Hero is someone who uses extraordinary abilities, called "super-powers," for the good of others. They might be born with these abilities, gain them with training, acquire them through accidents or experiments, or even use technology for an advantage.

## ARE THEY ALL HUMAN?

Not all of them. Most are humans from Earth, but a few are actually aliens from other worlds, including Thor and most of the Guardians of the Galaxy. Super Heroes can also be artificial life-forms, like the android Vision.

## WHO EXACTLY ARE THE AVENGERS?

Some (but not all) of these Super Heroes belong to a powerful team, known as the Avengers. The team's members work together and unite their strengths to protect the Earth from dangerous threats and villains.

## DO THE AVENGERS ALL GET ALONG?

It's complicated! The Avengers are thrown together because of dire circumstances, which makes for unconventional alliances. Strong personality flaws—like Hulk's volatile temper and Tony Stark's ego—put strain on friendships. Some members—like Scarlet Witch—even start out as foes of the Avengers and become allies later. And of course, sometimes arguments tear the team apart.

# WHO HAS THE TRICKY JOB OF TEAM LEADER?

Technically it's Captain America, but Tony Stark (Iron Man) often takes charge. Tony was only ever meant to be a consultant, but during the team's first battle, his management skills and company resources are indispensible. Nonetheless, Cap and Tony often seem like co-leaders, which leads to problems.

# SO CAN ANYONE JOIN?

Nope! Avengers candidates must be Super Heroes, and they must be invited. The team's founding members are Hulk, Captain America, Iron Man, Thor, Black Widow, and Hawkeye. By the end of *Avengers: Age of Ultron*, Scarlet Witch, Vision, War Machine, and Falcon become official members, while Hawkeye retires, Thor leaves Earth, and Hulk goes M.I.A.!

**The Avengers**
The original Avengers line-up faces an alien invasion during the Battle of New York.

Super Hero **Black Panther** fights for his family and peace in his country, Wakanda.

Cat burglar turned hero **Ant-Man** stops tech from falling into the wrong hands.

The **Avengers** are Earth's strongest defense against forces that wish to conquer or destroy it.

A Master of the Mystic Arts, **Doctor Strange** deals with some of the more supernatural threats facing Earth.

Far from Earth, the **Guardians of the Galaxy** are a bunch of fun-loving outlaws who fight on alien worlds.

*No one I know can run that fast or travel through time, so...*

# WHAT ARE SUPER-POWERS?

*The MCU's heroes and villains all have extraordinary talents. Some skills are gained through intense training and practice. Other abilities are endowed by technology or through some bizarre mishap. Certain characters are even born with supernatural powers. Here's a selection!*

### MYSTIC ARTS
Time and space travel, creating portals, wearing swishy robes, magic basically!

SPECIAL MENTION:
**DOCTOR STRANGE**

### COMBAT
Mean right hooks, crazy high kicks, Olympic-standard somersaults, hammer time.

SPECIAL MENTION:
**BLACK WIDOW**

### INTELLECT
Solving the world's problems, making cool new things, always thinking you're right.

SPECIAL MENTION:
**IRON MAN**

### SPEED
Zooming around, knocking out foes before they see you, never riding the bus again.

SPECIAL MENTION:
**QUICKSILVER**

## STRENGTH

Lifting cars, squishing cyborg space whales, manhandling helicopters.

SPECIAL MENTION:
**HULK**

## INTANGIBILITY

Walking through walls, floating on air, escaping being buried alive.

SPECIAL MENTION:
**VISION**

## DURABILITY

Never taking sick leave, being hard to injure, shielding your friends, growing a new you.

SPECIAL MENTION:
**GROOT**

## WEB-SLINGING

Swinging around the block, tripping up giants, sticking people to walls.

SPECIAL MENTION:
**SPIDER-MAN**

## FLIGHT

Swooping over big battles, catching falling friends, checking out the coolest views.

## SHRINKING

Sneaking into evil lairs, finding coins down the back of the couch, getting to ride ants.

SPECIAL MENTION:
**ANT-MAN**

*Some places look familiar, but others are otherworldly...*

# WHERE ARE THE MOVIES SET?

*These movies happen in lots of different places—and some of the locations are a bit odd. How many cities, countries, and worlds do I need to learn about?*

## ARE ALL THE FILMS SET IN THE SAME UNIVERSE?

Kind of! All MCU movies take place—at least partly—in the same universe. This is a pretty cool thing for fans, because it allows all of the movies to interconnect. One thing to bear in mind: While *Doctor Strange* is set primarily in this same universe, the characters do sometimes visit others!

## HOW DO THEY CONNECT?

Occasionally MCU movies make passing references to each other or share characters, but it's the big events (and their aftermath) that matter most. These include the Battles of New York (*Marvel's The Avengers*) and Sokovia (*Avengers: Age of Ultron*), the clash between the Avengers (*Captain America: Civil War*), and the conflict with the villain Thanos (*Marvel Studios' Avengers: Infinity War*).

## WHERE DO THINGS HAPPEN?

A lot of events happen in New York City, Washington D.C., and Southern California, but MCU movies can be set anywhere. Two important fictional countries are the European nation of Sokovia, and the African kingdom of Wakanda.

**NEW YORK CITY**
The "Big Apple" is often a base for the Avengers. It's also a prime target for alien invasions and mystical entities. Always lots to see here!

**WASHINGTON D.C.**
The U.S. capital hosts the intelligence agency S.H.I.E.L.D., sometimes making it the center of the action! Plus, Cap enjoys running around it.

**SOKOVIA**
This country in eastern Europe becomes a rallying cry for anti-Avengers sentiment, after it is destroyed during the carnage of a huge battle.

# WHY DOES SO MUCH STUFF HAPPEN ON THE MCU'S EARTH?

Many reasons! Some Super Heroes, like Ant-Man and Cap, are from Earth. Some villains believe Earth is an easy target, with little might. Ancient and powerful weapons that have found their way to Earth are also sought by ambitious extra-terrestrial beings, who would use them to dominate the universe!

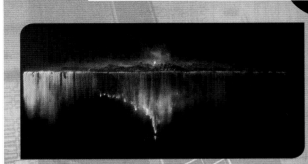

Thor calls the ethereal realm of **Asgard** home. It boasts elegant architecture and even has a shiny rainbow bridge.

# AND THERE ARE OTHER WORLDS, RIGHT?

Yes! Unearthly realms tend to concern Thor, the Guardians of the Galaxy, and Doctor Strange. Thor and the Guardians spend a great deal of time in space and on alien worlds, while Doctor Strange uses magic to open portals to other weird and wonderful dimensions.

It turns out that the MCU dimension is just one of an infinite number that make up the **Multiverse!**

# SUPER HERO BASES

**Tony Stark's mansion**
The swanky seaside home and personal laboratory of Tony Stark rests atop a cliff in California.

**New Avengers facility**
A group of ex-Stark Industries warehouses, converted into a new base and living quarters in upstate New York.

**New York Sanctum Sanctorum**
The mystical retreat of Doctor Strange. He relocates here after his epic battle in Hong Kong.

**Avengers Tower**
Also known as Stark Tower. It serves as the Avengers' New York operations base, until the rise of evil android Ultron.

**Pym Residence**
Hank Pym's manor in San Francisco serves as both a training facility and a base of operations for Ant-Man.

**Wakanda**
Black Panther's stunning remote kingdom is one of Earth's most technologically advanced nations.

*There are so many cool vehicles, weapons, and gadgets...*

# WHERE DOES ALL THE TECH COME FROM?

*Captain America's shield, Falcon's jet pack, Spider-Man's suit... businessman Tony Stark is at the center of the Avengers—is he responsible for all this advanced technology?*

**STARK TOWER**
Tony likes to be subtle...

## WHAT IS STARK INDUSTRIES?

Stark Industries is a multinational corporation owned by Tony Stark (Iron Man). Tony took over the company at age 21, after the deaths of his parents. The company's headquarters (not to be confused with Avengers Tower in Manhattan) is located in Los Angeles. The income from the company enables Tony to be a "billionaire playboy philanthropist."

## WHO CREATED THIS MEGA BUSINESS?

Stark Industries was founded by Tony's dad, Howard Stark, in 1939. Howard actually appears in several of the films. As a young man he is played by actor Dominic Cooper in *Captain America: The First Avenger*. Actor Gerard Sanders assumes the role in *Iron Man*. In *Ant-Man* and *Captain America: Civil War* he is portrayed by actor John Slattery.

## WHAT DOES STARK INDUSTRIES MAKE?

Most importantly, it builds Tony's Iron Man suits. It also manufactures industrial robots, vehicles, weapons, and munitions. Much of it is earmarked for the use of S.H.I.E.L.D. (an intelligence agency), the U.S. government, and the Avengers. This goes all the way back to Captain America's shield, which Howard built during World War II.

# IS STARK TECH ONLY USED BY THE GOOD GUYS?

Sadly, no. Sometimes, the weapons that the company makes fall into the wrong hands. Bombs built by Stark Industries are responsible for killing the parents of Quicksilver and Scarlet Witch, for example. Later, when Tony realizes a terrorist group known as The Ten Rings is using his weapons, he shuts down his firm's lucrative weapons division.

**Howard Stark** tried (and very much failed) to convince Hank Pym to share his research into shrinking particles.

# SO DOES EVERYONE USE STARK TECH?

Nope! Thor's hammer and the gear used by the Guardians of the Galaxy are alien in origin, while Black Panther's suit comes from the technologically advanced nation of Wakanda. Ant-Man's suit was developed by Howard's competitor, Hank Pym, and Doctor Strange's equipment is mystically powered.

Though Stark Tech appears advanced, the weapons of alien races like the **Chitauri** can make it seem primitive.

# WHO MADE WHAT?

**Captain America's shield**
This iconic shield is made from the Earth's rarest metal: vibranium. It was created by Howard Stark during WWII.

**Falcon's jet pack**
Officially known as the EXO-7, the current version of this prototype military wing suit was built specially for Falcon by Tony.

**Spider-Man's suit**
This advanced suit replaces Peter Parker's homemade original. Made by Tony, it boasts high-tech features, such as an A.I. assistant.

**Iron Man's suits**
There have been a LOT of Iron Man suits. All are lovingly designed and built by Tony himself, either at his Malibu home or Stark Tower.

**Ant-Man's suit**
Scientist Hank Pym created the Ant-Man suit during the Cold War. As the original Ant-Man, Hank used the suit to battle against the Soviets.

**Black Panther's suit**
This cool combat suit is lined with vibranium and was made in Wakanda. Like Cap's shield, the suit is almost indestructible.

*There are so many characters and so many movies...*

# WHICH ORDER SHOULD I WATCH THE FILMS IN?

*So all these movies tie together in one huge, awesome story. You can watch the movies in order of release date (moving Captain America: The First Avenger after Thor)—but if you want to follow the in-world story as it unfolds, you'll probably find this path the easiest!*

**1** CAPTAIN AMERICA: THE FIRST AVENGER (2011)

**2** IRON MAN (2008)

**3** THE INCREDIBLE HULK (2008)

IRON MAN 2 (2010)

**4**

**5** THOR (2011)

**6** MARVEL'S THE AVENGERS (2012)

**7** IRON MAN 3 (2013)

**8** THOR: THE DARK WORLD (2013)

**9** CAPTAIN AMERICA: THE WINTER SOLDIER (2014)

**10** GUARDIANS OF THE GALAXY (2014)

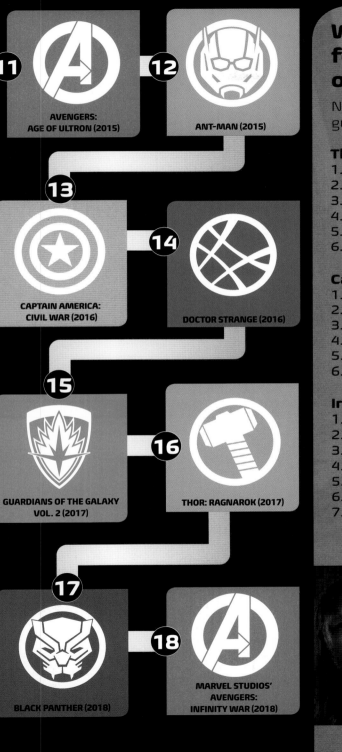

**11** AVENGERS: AGE OF ULTRON (2015)

**12** ANT-MAN (2015)

**13** CAPTAIN AMERICA: CIVIL WAR (2016)

**14** DOCTOR STRANGE (2016)

**15** GUARDIANS OF THE GALAXY VOL. 2 (2017)

**16** THOR: RAGNAROK (2017)

**17** BLACK PANTHER (2018)

**18** MARVEL STUDIOS' AVENGERS: INFINITY WAR (2018)

# What if I only want to follow the stories of one character?

No problem—here's a handy viewing guide to some key movies!

## Thor
1. *Thor*
2. *Marvel's The Avengers*
3. *Thor: The Dark World*
4. *Avengers: Age of Ultron*
5. *Thor: Ragnarok*
6. *Marvel Studios' Avengers: Infinity War*

## Captain America
1. *Captain America: The First Avenger*
2. *Marvel's The Avengers*
3. *Captain America: The Winter Soldier*
4. *Avengers: Age of Ultron*
5. *Captain America: Civil War*
6. *Marvel Studios' Avengers: Infinity War*

## Iron Man
1. *Iron Man*
2. *Iron Man 2*
3. *Marvel's The Avengers*
4. *Iron Man 3*
5. *Avengers: Age of Ultron*
6. *Captain America: Civil War*
7. *Marvel Studios' Avengers: Infinity War*

*There's a lot of material to digest in the movies themselves...*

# WHY SHOULD I STAY FOR THE CREDITS?

*So there are additional scenes hidden away in the credits of each movie. What will I find there and is it worth the wait?*

## Iron Man

Introduces Nick Fury and the Avengers Initiative.

## The Incredible Hulk

Tony Stark tells General Thaddeus Ross that a special team is being put together.

## Iron Man 2

Agent Coulson foreshadows Thor by revealing his hammer.

## Thor

Loki controls Selvig as he examines the Tesseract.

## Captain America: The First Avenger

Nick Fury gives Captain America an assignment.

## Marvel's The Avengers

1. The Other informs Thanos of Loki's defeat.
2. The Avengers eat at Shawarma Palace.

## Thor: The Dark World

1. Sif and Volstagg take the Aether to the Collector.
2. Thor returns to Earth to see Jane.

## Iron Man 3

Tony recounts his story to Bruce Banner.

## Thor: Ragnarok

1. A giant ship looms ominously above Thor and Loki's vessel.
2. The Grandmaster tries to talk his way out of danger.

## Guardians of the Galaxy Vol. 2

1. Kraglin practices with his new arrow.
2. Stakar reassembles his team.
3. Ayesha reveals Adam.
4. Star-Lord lectures adolescent Groot.
5. The Watchers walk away from Stan Lee.

## Doctor Strange

1. Doctor Strange questions Thor.
2. Mordo visits Jonathan Pangborn.

## Captain America: Civil War

1. Bucky receives asylum in Wakanda.
2. Peter Parker examines his new gear.

## Ant-Man

1. Hank Pym presents Hope van Dyne with the Wasp suit.
2. Captain America and Falcon discuss the Winter Soldier.

## Avengers: Age of Ultron

Thanos dons the Infinity Gauntlet.

## Guardians of the Galaxy

1. Baby Groot dances.
2. The Collector sits in his ruined museum.

## Captain America: The Winter Soldier

"If we can't protect the Earth, you can be damned well sure we'll avenge it!"

TONY STARK

# PHASE ONE

## CAPTAIN AMERICA:
### THE FIRST AVENGER

**24**

# THE ONE WHERE...
It's the 1940s! Wimpy Steve Rogers is turned into the mighty Captain America. He joins the war and defeats a guy with a red face, but gets stuck in an ice cube.

# IRON MAN

**30**

# THE ONE WHERE...
Playboy Tony Stark is captured by bad guys. He creates a flashy suit of armor to escape and prevents a corporate takeover by a nasty co-worker. Iron Man is born!

# IRON MAN 2

**36**

# THE ONE WHERE...
Tony is out of the Super Hero closet. He faces a bitter villain with whips, but Tony's buddy War Machine and super-spy Black Widow help defeat the bad guy.

# THOR

**42**

# THE ONE WHERE...
Muscly Norse god Thor is banished to Earth for bad behavior. He finds love, stops his scheming brother, Loki, and becomes worthy enough to wield a magic hammer.

# MARVEL'S THE AVENGERS

**48**

# THE ONE WHERE...
A gang of Super Heroes assemble to save the world! They beat pesky Loki and protect New York from an army of weird-looking aliens and space whales.

# CAPTAIN AMERICA:
## THE FIRST AVENGER

## AN OVERVIEW

Captain America: The First Avenger *premiered in July 2011. It was the first* Captain America *movie, and the fifth movie released in the MCU, but the earliest in the in-universe chronological timeline.*

### LOST AND FOUND

In the present-day Arctic, explorers discover an aircraft buried in the ice. Inside, they find a distinctive round shield. In another scene, set in Tønsberg, Norway in 1942, Nazi officer (and Hydra leader) Johann Schmidt steals a supernatural relic named the Tesseract from an old church.

### TAMPERING WITH THE TESSERACT

Meanwhile, in Germany, Schmidt and Dr. Arnim Zola use the Tesseract to power futuristic weapons, planning to use them for world domination. Schmidt's ambitions pit him against his own Nazi regime, from which he plans to break away. Schmidt is informed of Dr. Erskine's location in the U.S., and sends Hydra agent Heinz Kruger to assassinate him.

### TIME TO BE A SUPER-SOLDIER

In New York City, 1942, Steve Rogers is once again rejected from military recruitment due to health issues. When he and best friend Bucky Barnes attend the Stark Expo, Rogers tries to enlist yet again. Dr. Abraham Erskine overhears Steve talking to Bucky about his desire to serve, and recruits him into the Strategic Scientific Reserve (S.S.R.) as part of its Super-Soldier program, overseen by Colonel Chester Phillips and Agent Peggy Carter. Success!

### CREATING CAPTAIN AMERICA

At a secret government facility, Erskine administers the Super-Soldier serum to Steve and places him in a metal capsule, where he is bombarded with vita-rays. Transformation time! Steve emerges much taller and stronger, but Kruger then attacks and kills Erskine. Steve pursues Kruger but the Hydra agent kills himself before he can be questioned.

**Steve hates bullies, and the Nazis are the biggest bullies around, but all of his attempts to enlist fail.**

### BORED AND FRUSTRATED

With little hope of continuing the Super-Soldier program after Erskine's death, the U.S. government gives Steve a showy costume, bestows him with the nickname "Captain America" (or "Cap"), and orders him to promote the sale of war bonds. He finds the work disappointing and somewhat degrading.

## UNCOVERING RED SKULL

While on a show tour to the frontline in Italy, Cap discovers Bucky is missing in action. He has Peggy and businessman Howard Stark fly him behind enemy lines to search for his friend. Steve discovers Bucky and other allied soldiers held captive in Schmidt's Hydra fortress. While escaping, Cap confronts Schmidt, who removes his mask to reveal his horrific true face as Red Skull.

## LOSING BUCKY

Cap and Bucky form a team known as the Howling Commandos to fight Hydra. Howard Stark provides them with high-tech weaponry, including a round vibranium shield for Cap. They successfully capture Zola from a Hydra train, but Bucky appears to fall to his death. Zola is interrogated, and reveals the location of Schmidt's final stronghold.

**The Howling Commandos prepare to zip-wire onto a Hydra train carrying Arnim Zola. They don't realize they're heading into a trap!**

## CAPTAIN'S SACRIFICE

Steve's team infiltrates the Hydra base, but Schmidt takes off in an aircraft armed with weapons of mass destruction intended for U.S. cities. Steve climbs inside as it takes off and fights Red Skull. During the conflict, Red Skull tries to use the Tesseract, but in handling it he disappears in a beam of energy. The Tesseract then falls into the sea. Noble Steve crashes the plane to stop it from reaching its targets.

## TO THE FUTURE!

Steve wakes up in a 1940s-era hospital room, but notices the "live" baseball game on the radio is one he's already seen. Realizing something is wrong, Steve runs outside and finds himself in present-day Times Square. Nick Fury, director of S.H.I.E.L.D., tells him he has been sleeping for almost 70 years.

# GOOD GUYS

**CAPTAIN AMERICA (STEVE ROGERS)**
American hero, Capsicle

**BUCKY BARNES**
Comrade-in-arms, plummeting pal

**PEGGY CARTER**
Brave soldier with a broken heart

**HOWLING COMMANDOS**
Best of the best, Cap's groupies

**DR. ABRAHAM ERSKINE**
Great doctor, bad bullet-dodger

**HOWARD STARK**
Entrepreneur, Tony Stark's dad

# BAD GUYS

**RED SKULL (JOHANN SCHMIDT)**
Red-head Hydra honcho

**DR. ARNIM ZOLA**
Doctor of evil, Hydra fanatic

*I know he wears red, white, and blue and carries a shield...*

# SO WHO IS CAPTAIN AMERICA?

*Clearly the guy is patriotic and I think he's been around for a long time. But where did Captain America come from? And is he a soldier or a vigilante?*

**CAPTAIN AMERICA**
The first Avenger

## WAS CAPTAIN AMERICA ALWAYS A SUPER HERO?

No, he wasn't! However, Steve Rogers was a brave, honorable, and patriotic young man before he became Captain America. The Brooklyn native applies many times to join the U.S. military and fight in World War II, but he is always rejected due to health problems and his frail physique.

## HOW DOES STEVE ROGERS BECOME CAPTAIN AMERICA?

Steve meets Dr. Abraham Erskine, who allows him to enlist and volunteer for the Super-Soldier program, more formally known as Project Rebirth. Dr. Erskine administers Steve with a top-secret serum and exposes him to "vita-rays," all of which transform the frail recruit into a soldier of physical perfection. Hooray!

*"Are you ready to follow 'Captain America' into the jaws of death?"*

*STEVE ROGERS*

# WHY DOES DR. ERSKINE CHOOSE STEVE?

Erskine believes that only someone who knows what it's like to be weak will be able to wield the strength of a Super-Soldier with humility. Or, in other words, because weedy Steve is a person who bravely stands up to bullies, even though he always gets beaten to a pulp!

# WHAT IS HIS MISSION?

At first, that's uncertain. Steve was supposed to be just the first of many Super-Soldiers, but Dr. Erskine is assassinated by Hydra agent Heinz Kruger—and with him dies the secret of the Super-Soldier serum. The U.S. military has no strategic use for just one Super-Soldier! After his friend Bucky gets captured by Hydra, though, things take an explosive turn.

# HOW DID STEVE END UP IN THE PRESENT DAY?

It's a long story (which, luckily for you, we summarized on the previous pages), but basically Captain America climbs aboard a Hydra plane on its way to drop weapons of mass destruction on the U.S. In order to save the country, he has to heroically crash the plane in the Arctic. Cap wakes up in the present day, presumably having been preserved in the ice by his hardy Super-Soldier physiology, and is then rescued by the S.H.I.E.L.D. agents whom we saw in the movie's prologue.

Steve leaves the **vita-ray chamber** as a new man—literally! He is now faster and stronger than any normal human.

You may not know it yet, but **James Buchanan "Bucky" Barnes** goes on to play a crucial role in the MCU. Exciting!

S.S.R. agent **Peggy Carter** is a key member of Project Rebirth. She trains Steve, and later falls in love with him.

# WHAT IS HYDRA?

*I've seen a guy wearing a red Halloween mask and people wearing a symbol that looks like a skull octopus. Who are these guys and why is Captain America fighting them?*

**HYDRA SYMBOL**
Tentacles and bones

## WHO IS THE GUY WITH THE RED FACE?

The man who looks like he's eaten too many red-hot chilli peppers is Johann Schmidt, the head of Hydra. He is known as Red Skull for obvious reasons. His "normal face" is actually the red one! His true appearance is revealed during a confrontation with Captain America late in the movie.

## WHAT ON EARTH HAPPENED TO HIM?

Schmidt stole an earlier version of Dr. Erskine's Super-Soldier serum and injected it into himself, hoping to gain super-powers. Obviously the experiment didn't go well! Though it endowed Schmidt with superior physical abilities, it left him horribly disfigured.

> *"Quite simply, gentlemen, I have harnessed the power of the gods."*
>
> *JOHANN SCHMIDT*

# AND WHAT IS HYDRA?

Hydra is the Nazi science division, with secret bases, factories, and agents in place all over the world. It is run almost like a cult, with its agents more loyal to Red Skull and Hydra than to Hitler himself.

# SO IS SCHMIDT A NAZI?

Schmidt starts out as a Nazi, but he and Hydra work independently of the regime. Ambitious Schmidt comes to believe that Hydra can no longer flourish in Hitler's shadow. Once Schmidt obtains the Tesseract, it's time for a career change. He turns against the Nazis and includes Berlin among his targets for destruction.

# WHAT IS THE TESSERACT?

The Tesseract is a mysterious object that Red Skull retrieves from an ancient tomb in Norway. With it, he and his assistant Dr. Arnim Zola power highly advanced weapons, which they plan to use to take over the world. These plans fall apart when Red Skull is defeated by Captain America.

# YAY! IS RED SKULL DEAD?

That's not entirely clear! During his final confrontation with Captain America, Red Skull handles the Tesseract with his bare hands and is vaporized. Did it really kill him, or did it merely transport him elsewhere? We'll have to wait and see how things unfold!

The cube-shaped **Tesseract** is actually just a containment vessel for one of the vastly powerful Infinity Stones.

**Dr. Arnim Zola** is a brilliant but amoral scientist, used by Schmidt to create weapons for Hydra's global conquest.

The Tesseract-powered weapons are devastating. Schmidt uses a **prototype cannon** to vaporize two SS officers.

# IRON MAN

Iron Man *debuted at #1 at the U.S. box office in 2008—and kicked off the entire MCU. The movie starred Robert Downey Jr. as Tony Stark (Iron Man) and was directed by Jon Favreau, who also plays Tony's driver, Happy Hogan.*

### RUDE INTERRUPTION

While in Afghanistan demonstrating his new missile to the U.S. military, billionaire businessman Tony and his convoy are attacked by a terrorist group, known as The Ten Rings. Just before it explodes and nearly kills him, Tony notices a bomb bearing his company's name—Stark Industries.

### BUSTING OUT

Tony builds a small but very powerful generator, called an Arc Reactor, to replace the magnet in his chest and power a metal suit, which the pair plan to use to escape. Selfless Yinsen later sacrifices himself to give Tony time to complete the suit. Tony fights his way out of the camp and flies away, but crashes in the desert, where he is rescued by his friend, Lieutenant Colonel James "Rhodey" Rhodes.

### CHILD GENIUS

Three days earlier, at an awards show in Las Vegas, a presentation details Tony's life so far. He was a child prodigy in engineering, computer science, and electronics. Sadly, Tony's parents were killed in a car accident when he was 17. Aged 21, he took control of his father's company, with the help of his father's business partner, Obadiah Stane. Today, the company continues to deal in technology, especially weapons.

Instead of a missile, Dr. Ho Yinsen helps Tony construct the Mark I suit out of scraps of metal.

### CAPTURED!

Back in the present, Tony is captured and held at The Ten Rings' camp. There, fellow captive Dr. Ho Yinsen installs an electromagnet over Tony's heart, to stop bomb shrapnel embedded in his chest killing him. Raza, The Ten Rings' leader, promises Tony freedom in exchange for building them a missile. Both prisoners suspect this is a lie...

### PERFECTING IRON MAN

When Tony returns home to the U.S., he announces that he is closing the weapons division of his company, which causes friction with Stane. Tony secretly builds a better replacement Arc Reactor and a more advanced Iron Man suit in his own private workshop.

## BACK TO AFGHANISTAN

Tony learns that his company is still selling weapons to The Ten Rings, and that they are being used to blitz Yinsen's former village. When Tony confronts his partner, Stane reveals he is working against him. Tony then flies off to Afghanistan to intervene and save the villagers. On the flight home, two Air Force jets attack Tony and he is forced to tell Rhodey that he is Iron Man.

To escape the Air Force attack, Tony hides on one of the jets' undercarriages and calls Rhodey for help.

## PEPPER ON THE CASE

Meanwhile, The Ten Rings recover Tony's original prototype suit and show it to Stane. Stane then builds a massive new suit based on the wreckage. Tony grows suspicious of Stane and asks his assistant Pepper Potts to copy Stane's computer records. In the process, she discovers Stane originally hired The Ten Rings to kill Tony. Pepper then gives the files to S.H.I.E.L.D. agent Phil Coulson.

## REMOVING THE STANE

Stane traps Tony and takes the Arc Reactor from his chest to power his new suit. Near death, Tony is able to re-install his old Arc Reactor. When S.H.I.E.L.D. agents try to arrest Stane, he emerges in his new armor and tries to kill everyone. Tony tries to stop Stane in an epic fight, but Tony's suit is limited by his old low-power reactor. In desperation, Tony tells Pepper to overload the jumbo Arc Reactor in the Stark Industries building below. The blast knocks Stane into the reactor and kills him. At a press conference the next day, Tony announces to the world that he is Iron Man.

> "Let's face it, this is not the worst thing you've caught me doing."
> · TONY STARK TO PEPPER POTTS

# GOOD GUYS

**IRON MAN (TONY STARK)**
Metal hero with heart

**PEPPER POTTS**
Faithful assistant, prospective life partner

**DR. HO YINSEN**
Selfless doctor, good samaritan

**HAPPY HOGAN**
Great driver (even better director)

**AGENT PHIL COULSON**
Gentleman, secret agent

# BAD GUYS

**OBADIAH STANE**
War profiteer, Iron Monger

**RAZA HAMIDMI AL-WAZAR**
The Ten Rings' leader, sole survivor

# WHY THE ARMOR?

*Obviously the armor protects him from something, but why does Iron Man need it if he's a Super Hero?*

**TONY STARK**
Man of iron

## WHO IS IRON MAN?

Iron Man is actually the billionaire Tony Stark. Underneath that armor, Tony is just a normal guy without any special powers. At the end of the first *Iron Man* movie, Tony reveals his identity as Iron Man to the entire world. He prefers to be transparent (and show off!)

## SO WHAT CAN THE IRON MAN SUIT DO?

The Iron Man suit allows Tony to fly, which means he can travel far on a whim, and its armor is strong enough to protect him from just about any kind of impact. The suit is also equipped with weapons in the palms of its hands, and is networked with a personal artificial intelligence assistant.

## HOW'D THIS ALL START?

Tony travels to Afghanistan to show his company's new Jericho missile to the U.S. military, but gets kidnapped by a terrorist organization named The Ten Rings. Tony is forced to build one of the deadly missiles for his captors.

Mark XLIII suit

# WHEN DOES HE BUILD HIS FIRST ARMOR?

Instead of a missile, Tony uses the tools at his disposal to build an iron suit, equipped with a jet pack and flamethrowers, and fights his way out of the prison where he is being held. However, he is forced to leave his damaged suit behind. The ordeal causes Tony to rethink his company and make some big changes when he gets home.

# SO TONY HAS A CHANGE OF HEART (SO TO SPEAK)?

Absolutely. During his captivity with The Ten Rings, Tony discovers that the weapons they use are made by his own company. As a result, Tony decides to abruptly shut down Stark Industries' weapons division—its most profitable venture—which is a bit of a shocker for the company's board of directors, and Tony's business partner, Obadiah Stane.

The **Mark III** armor is the first of Tony's suits to have the iconic red-and-yellow color scheme. Definitely a trendsetter.

A contemporary of Tony's father, **Obadiah Stane** has little respect for the younger Stark and his playboy antics.

## WHO IS TONY STARK?

The man inside the suit is not obvious Super Hero material. Until his kidnapping, Tony, although a genius, is also vain, arrogant, and dismissive of others—a spoiled rich kid who inherited his company and fortune from his father. Although his experiences in the desert change him for the better, occasionally Tony's old self still comes to the surface.

*I see a glowing circle in Iron Man's chest...*

# WHAT'S UP WITH TONY'S HEART?

*He looks like some kind of cyborg. Do those sparkly lights in his chest give Iron Man special abilities?*

## HAS TONY RECEIVED AN INJURY?

Yes, a serious one. After blowing up a hillside in a missile demo for the U.S. military, Tony's caravan is attacked by The Ten Rings. Just before he is critically wounded and knocked out in an explosion, Tony sees a bomb land beside him, labeled "Stark Industries."

## SO, COULD HE DIE?

Indeed—he very nearly does die! Shrapnel damages and weakens Tony's heart. At this stage, it isn't possible to remove all of the shrapnel from Tony's chest, and it slowly moves toward his heart. Take note— this unsettling reality remains a significant vulnerability for Tony in the future.

Mark I suit

## THEN WHO HELPS HIM?

Doctor Ho Yinsen is a surgeon, also held captive by The Ten Rings. He operates on Tony and saves his life. Yinsen hooks up a temporary electromagnet to keep the remaining shrapnel in Tony's chest from penetrating his heart. He also helps Tony build the first Iron Man suit and even sacrifices himself so Tony can escape.

# BUT WHAT'S THAT THING IN TONY'S CHEST?

Tony builds a miniature power source called an Arc Reactor, or RT (short for Reactor) to keep his heart pumping and prevent the shrapnel in his chest from moving. This is the glowing ring sticking out of his ribcage. It also powers his armor suit.

**PARANOID PARTNER**
After returning from Afghanistan, Tony shows the RT in his chest to his business partner (and soon-to-be foe) Obadiah Stane.

# SO WHAT DOES TONY DO NOW?

After escaping, Tony wants to devote his company to developing the RT's potential, instead of selling weapons. He secretly creates a new, more powerful RT for his chest, and a more advanced Iron Man suit to fight groups like The Ten Rings. This causes tension with his partner, who wants to know what Tony is really up to.

## THE TEN RINGS

The Ten Rings is a terrorist group shrouded in mystery. Dedicated to destroying world order, it is supposedly led by a shadowy figure known as the Mandarin. The team that captures Tony is commanded by Raza Hamidmi Al-Wazar.

Raza

# IRON MAN 2

## AN OVERVIEW

*The second thrilling* Iron Man *movie arrived in 2010. It introduced two new villains: sinister Ivan Vanko and slimy Justin Hammer. Another future Avenger is also introduced: the deadly Black Widow, played by Scarlett Johansson.*

### GRIEF AND PLOTTING

News of Tony Stark's identity as Iron Man reaches Russia. There, physicist Ivan Vanko and his father Anton watch Tony's press conference on TV. Upset by what he hears, Anton passes away. Ivan grieves his father's death as he begins constructing his own version of the RT to power a special suit. Ominous...

### MENACE IN MONACO

During a business trip, Tony's impending death makes him reckless and on a whim he enters the Monaco Grand Prix race. Suddenly, Ivan Vanko appears and attacks him, wielding electric whips. Pepper and Happy deliver the Iron Man suit to Tony, allowing him to defeat Vanko, who is arrested. Having witnessed the events, Hammer is so impressed by Vanko that he has Vanko's death faked in prison, and breaks him out.

### DOOM AND GLOOM

Six months later, Tony shows off his company's innovations at the Stark Expo. After, Tony is pressured to turn over his Iron Man suits to the government during a U.S. Senate hearing, but refuses. Tony's friend, Rhodey, is forced to give evidence that dangerous groups may be copying Stark technology. Tony's business rival Justin Hammer argues the Iron Man tech should be confiscated so his company can oversee its development for the military. Later, a dark reality dawns on Tony that the palladium core of the RT in his chest is actually poisoning him. Tony prepares for his demise by making his assistant Pepper Potts the CEO of Stark Industries, though he doesn't explain why. In turn, Pepper hires Natalie Rushman as Tony's new assistant.

Vanko interrupts the Grand Prix as "Whiplash," attacking Tony in a vicious assault.

### BIRTHDAY BASH AND SMASH

Tony celebrates what he thinks will be his last ever birthday. Rhodey arrives at the party to find Tony drunk and misbehaving while wearing his Iron Man suit. A disgusted Rhodey dons the old Mark II armor and they fight it out, trashing Tony's home. It ends in a draw and Rhodey leaves to take the armor to the Air Force, only to find Hammer has been awarded charge of its development.

> ## "I told you I don't want to join your super-secret boy band."
> *TONY STARK TO NICK FURY*

## LUNCH DATE

Nick Fury meets a hungover Tony in a diner and reveals that Natalie is actually S.H.I.E.L.D. agent Natasha Romanoff, aka Black Widow. Fury explains that Anton Vanko co-invented the RT with Tony's father, Howard, but when Anton betrayed him, Howard had him deported. Anton ended up in a Russian gulag.

## THE PROBLEM AT THE CORE

Natasha gives Tony a serum that eliminates the symptoms of palladium poisoning. This gives Tony the time and energy he needs to find a replacement core for his RT. He discovers a clue in an old video recording from his dad, leading Tony to develop an entirely new atomic element and solve the problem.

## HAMMER EXPO-SED

Hammer unveils his new military drones. Rhodey leads them in his War Machine suit—secretly modified by Vanko. Tony realizes Vanko and Hammer are colluding and tries to warn Rhodey, but Vanko takes remote control of both the drones and Rhodey's armor. Natasha breaks into Hammer HQ to restore control of Rhodey's armor to him. Tony and Rhodey fight the drones and Vanko, who has a new armored suit. Facing defeat, Vanko ends the fight by self-destructing.

Iron Man and War Machine join forces against an army of Hammer's drones that are under Vanko's control.

## GOOD GUYS

**IRON MAN
(TONY STARK)**
Flying Super Hero,
dead man walking

**PEPPER POTTS**
Powerful CEO,
Tony's life coach

**WAR MACHINE
(RHODEY RHODES)**
Tony's best friend,
War Machine

**BLACK WIDOW
(NATASHA ROMANOFF)**
Lightning-fast reflexes,
big fan of gadgets

**NICK FURY**
Keeps an eye on
national security

**HAPPY HOGAN**
Life-saving driver,
questionable right hook

## BAD GUYS

**WHIPLASH (IVAN VANKO)**
Mechanical genius
with a grudge

**JUSTIN HAMMER**
Rival CEO, disco-
dancing slimeball

# WHAT IS WRONG WITH TONY?

*Tony Stark is hosting wild parties and driving in ridiculous races. Is he having a mid-life crisis? Do Super Heroes go bad?*

**POISONED TONY**
Iron Man on the edge

## WHAT IS THE SOURCE OF TONY'S PROBLEM?

It all boils down to the RT in Tony's chest. The RT is keeping him alive, but Tony has realized that its palladium core is poisoning his blood and slowly killing him. Try as he might, Tony can't find a replacement material to fuel the RT and solve his problem.

## BUT WHY IS TONY SO RECKLESS?

Tony knows that since he can't replace the core, he will soon die. Which really sucks... So, he decides to make the most of things by partying and taking crazy risks. In the process he neglects his company, but fortunately his faithful assistant, Pepper Potts, steps in for him.

## HOW DOES PEPPER STEP IN FOR HIM?

Knowing his impending death means he must find a replacement to run Stark Industries, Tony makes Pepper Potts the new CEO of his company. Pepper hires Natalie Rushman as Tony's new assistant, but she turns out to be keeping a big secret...

## THAT'S EXCITING! WHAT IS SHE HIDING?

Fortunately for Tony, Natalie turns out to be S.H.I.E.L.D. Agent Natasha Romanoff (Black Widow). She gives Tony an injection that removes the symptoms of his palladium poisoning, and a box of Tony's father's old research. The injection buys him enough time to untangle his father's research, and create an entirely new element to replace the palladium. This isn't his only problem, though.

## SO WHAT *ELSE* IS GOING WRONG?

A Russian engineer named Ivan Vanko accuses Tony of living off a legacy stolen from Vanko's father, Anton. It turns out that Anton co-invented the original RT with Tony's father. After getting caught in some shady business, Vanko's father ended up spending his life in a Russian prison, and now the younger Vanko wants revenge!

Natasha Romanoff uses her exceptional **martial arts skills** to break into Hammer Industries headquarters.

**Vanko** and his **pet parrot** threaten Tony in a phone call. Vanko says he will avenge Anton by destroying Stark Industries.

Tony discovers his dad's diorama of the 1974 Stark Expo is really a diagram for the structure of a **new element**.

# WHO IS WAR MACHINE?

*I know who Iron Man is, but I see another guy running around in a metal suit, fighting lots of robots too. How do I tell them apart?*

**LEAVING A MARK...**
Tony keeps his suits on display in his workshop at home. Marks I–IV are shown here, with the Mark II armor second from left.

## HOW MANY SUITS ARE THERE?

Tony Stark built three Iron Man suits in the first film. By the end of *Iron Man 2*, he has a total of six. Each design is called a "Mark," numbered Mark I through Mark VI. Each flashy upgrade tends to be more advanced than the last.

## SO WHO IS WEARING THE SILVER ARMOR?

Tony Stark's close friend Lieutenant Colonel James "Rhodey" Rhodes puts on Tony's Mark II prototype armor, assuming the code name: "War Machine." In the first *Iron Man* film he is played by actor Terrence Howard. In *Iron Man 2* and thereafter he is played by actor Don Cheadle.

James Rhodes

## WHY HAVE TONY AND RHODEY FALLEN OUT?

The U.S. government pressures Rhodey to confiscate Tony's armor so the military can use it. Rhodey defends his pal's reckless behavior, but when he finds Tony drunk while wearing the Iron Man suit at his birthday party, Rhodey has enough and puts on the Mark II suit. Glass shatters in their epic duel!

## SO WHO WINS?

Neither. It ends in a draw, so angry Rhodey retreats and delivers the Mark II armor to the U.S. Air Force. However, he's upset to learn that Tony's smug business rival, Justin Hammer, has contracted with the government to use the suit as a prototype to develop similar technology. Hammer's plans don't work out, though!

## WHAT GOES WRONG WITH HAMMER'S SCHEME?

Hammer holds Ivan Vanko as a virtual prisoner, demanding the Russian build Iron Man suits for him. However, Vanko builds robot soldiers instead and one armored suit for himself, thus hijacking the whole operation. It culminates in Vanko's personal battle against Iron Man and War Machine.

**SHADY BUSINESS**
After breaking Vanko out of prison, Hammer offers him a deal over dinner—Vanko will keep his freedom if he builds armored suits for Hammer Industries.

# THOR

*Director Kenneth Branagh delivered the first Thor movie in 2011. The film introduced the title character played by actor Chris Hemsworth, Natalie Portman as Dr. Jane Foster, Tom Hiddleston as Loki, and Anthony Hopkins as Odin.*

## CORONATION CANCELED

Just as Thor, prince of Asgard, is about to ascend to the throne in a coronation ceremony, some Frost Giants sneak into King Odin's treasure vault and try to steal a weapon of mass destruction, the Casket of Ancient Winters. An enchanted mechanical guardian known as the Destroyer stops them, but the event raises Thor's ire and postpones his crowning. Cue much shouting.

> **"What?! He was freaking me out!"**
>
> DARCY TO JANE AND ERIK ABOUT TASERING THOR

Odin is dressed up in his finest armor, with a matching eyepatch, to coronate Thor.

## BANISHMENT WITH A BACK DOOR

Odin is furious with Thor for destroying the delicate peace treaty between Asgard and the Frost Giants. He strips Thor of his power and banishes him to Earth. Not without mercy, Odin puts a spell on Thor's hammer, Mjolnir, and throws it after Thor. Odin secretly hopes that the hammer's new enchantment will provide an opportunity for Thor to redeem himself.

## FROSTY RECEPTION

Against Odin's orders, Thor, his friends—Sif and the Warriors Three (named Volstagg, Hogun, and Fandral)—and his brother, Loki, make a plan. They go to the realm of Jotunheim via the Bifrost bridge to get answers from the Frost Giants' king, Laufey. He implies that an Asgardian traitor aided the Frost Giants, and goads Thor into an epic fight. Thor and friends nearly meet their doom, but Odin arrives and saves them in the nick of time.

## HAMMER AND S.H.I.E.L.D.

Thor is discovered on Earth by astrophysicist Dr. Jane Foster, her mentor Dr. Erik Selvig, and their intern, Darcy. S.H.I.E.L.D. Agent Phil Coulson commandeers all of Jane's research, leaving her enraged. Thor learns that S.H.I.E.L.D. has found his hammer and so breaks into their facility, but finds he is unable to lift Mjolnir. S.H.I.E.L.D. takes a distraught Thor into custody.

## LOKI'S BETRAYAL

Loki finds out that he is actually adopted. He was abandoned as a baby by his true father, Laufey. Odin took pity on Loki and adopted him. Loki confronts Odin, but the stress of losing both sons sends Odin into the Odinsleep. With Odin in a coma from which he may never awake, Loki takes the throne. Thor's friends respond by disobeying Loki and traveling to Earth in hopes of bringing Thor home.

## DESTROYER

Noting their defiance, Loki sends the Destroyer to Earth after the four friends to eliminate them all. Thor and Jane evacuate the local townspeople while his Asgardian friends try to stop the Destroyer, without success. In an effort to save everyone, Thor offers himself up to the Destroyer, who deals what seems a fatal blow. As he lays dying, Thor is finally deemed worthy to reclaim his hammer and is restored to his full power. Thor defeats the giant metal sentry, and then he and his friends head home to Asgard, promising Jane he will return.

Sif is ready to die a warrior's death attacking the Destroyer, and live on in stories. Thor persuades Sif to live and tell the stories herself.

## RAINBOW BRIDGE

Loki reveals to Laufey that he is the one who allowed the Frost Giants into Asgard during the coronation. He now invites Laufey to come to Asgard and slay his helpless father, Odin. However, Loki betrays Laufey when he arrives, killing the Frost Giant in an effort to prove himself to Odin. Thor returns to finds Loki in the process of using the power of the Bifrost bridge to annihilate Laufey's world. To prevent Loki from destroying an entire race, Thor destroys the Bifrost bridge (and with it, the Asgardians' ability to visit other realms). Odin wakes just in time to save his sons from falling into the void created by the destruction, but rebellious Loki lets go and vanishes.

## GOOD GUYS

**THOR**
Don't call him a princess

**DR. JANE FOSTER**
Leading astrophysicist, cleverest in the realm

**SIF**
Self-made warrior, loyal friend

**HEIMDALL**
Gate-keeper, Loki-hater

**ODIN**
Likes naptime and big thrones

**DR. ERIK SELVIG**
Sceptical professor, Jane's mentor

## BAD GUYS

**LOKI**
Green with envy, blue underneath

**LAUFEY**
Cold as ice, ugly as hell

*I think I've heard of this guy, and not only from comic books...*

# IS THOR A GOD?

*His swaggering step and bulging muscles make Thor look like a knight in shining armor. But besides his good looks, what is this super-powered show-off all about?*

**MJOLNIR**
Hammer time!

## SO IS THOR SUPPOSED TO BE A DEITY?

Thor is known as the God of Thunder. He and his family (his father Odin, mother Frigga, and younger brother Loki) refer to themselves as gods because of their extraordinary lifespan, mighty fortitude, and ample super-powers. Yet Odin tells Loki, "We are not gods. We are born, we live, we die, just as humans do." So, you could think of Asgardians as super-powered aliens with a humility deficit.

## IS THOR *THE* THOR? LIKE, VIKING THOR?

According to Odin, ancient humans knew they weren't alone in the universe. In 965AD, Odin and his army waged war in Norway to protect humans from the evil Frost Giants. Many characters, places, and objects from Norse mythology appear in *Thor*, implying Earth's legends were inspired by the Asgardians.

> *"Whosoever holds this hammer, if he be worthy, shall possess the power of Thor."*
>
> *ODIN*

# WHAT ARE HIS POWERS?

Apart from his extraordinary strength and durability, Thor can also summon lightning, though at this point only via his trusty hammer. You might be wondering why he calls himself the God of Thunder if he's actually wielding lightning, but it's best to disregard that little discrepancy as mere semantics!

# HE HAS A HAMMER... IS HE A CARPENTER?

Er, no. Thor adores his magical hammer, which he believes only he can wield. It even has a name: Mjolnir (but it's funnier to call it "myeh myeh," as Jane's intern Darcy does). Thor takes great pride in chucking it at hoards of enemies, and recalling it from any distance by simply stretching out a hand. He can also fly by hanging onto the strap as he throws it, pulling him into the air. It beats getting the bus.

# IS THOR REALLY THE ONLY ONE TO WIELD IT?

When Thor disobeys his father, Odin puts an enchantment on Mjolnir so only someone worthy may lift it—which at the time, excludes a moody Thor. Even when he redeems himself though, Thor later discovers he isn't the only one with the ability to lift it. In future films, Captain America, Vision, and Hela all tamper with it to varying degrees.

# WHERE DOES THOR COME FROM?

Asgard is the home of Thor and his people. It's not a round planet like Earth. Rather, Asgard is flat, with a mountainous island at the center, surrounded by seas that drop off into space. Kind of like a magical asteroid with gravity and a livable atmosphere. Asgard is one of the Nine Realms (planets). The other eight are: Svartalfheim, Vanaheim, Midgard (Earth), Jotunheim, Nidavell Niflheim, Muspelheim, and Alfheim.

Tourist hotspot alert. The **Asgardian Palace** is the home of the royal family, and stands in the center of Asgard.

# WHAT IS THOR UP TO ON EARTH?

*Thor left the paradise of Asgard for the drudgery of Earth. How did he get so far from home? Did he accidentally swing his hammer too hard?*

## DID THOR GET LOST?

When Frost Giants try to steal a powerful artifact from the Royal Palace, Thor has a massive tantrum. He, Loki, and his friends retaliate by invading the Frost Giants' realm of Jotunheim, violating a peace treaty, and igniting a new war. Thor's recklessness enrages Odin, who banishes him to Earth through a wormhole. Thor is found by scientist Dr. Jane Foster and her team when she accidentally hits him with her van.

## WHAT DOES THOR DO NOW HE'S ON EARTH?

At first, Thor tries in vain to retrieve Mjolnir, but later resigns himself to life on Earth. It's not all doom and gloom, though—Thor discovers coffee, as well as a romance developing between himself and Jane. Trouble beckons, however, when Odin falls into a coma known as "Odinsleep," and Loki pounces on the opportunity to take control of Asgard. Thor's closest friends travel to Earth to warn him.

> **"This drink. I like it... ANOTHER!"**
>
> *THOR, ON COFFEE*

# HOW DOES HE SET THINGS RIGHT?

Loki sends the Destroyer to Earth to finish off Thor. Stripped of his powers, Thor nobly sacrifices himself to save his friends. At the edge of death, he is deemed worthy by Odin and his powers are restored. Upon vanquishing the Destroyer, Thor returns to Asgard to stop Loki, who seeks to obliterate Jotunheim, using both the Bifrost and the Casket of Ancient Winters.

# ERM, JUST WHAT EXACTLY ARE THOSE?

The Bifrost is a crystal "rainbow bridge" that draws its power from Asgard to transport people between the Nine Realms, including Earth. It is guarded by the Asgardian known as Heimdall. If left open too long, the Bifrost's energy can destroy a planet. The Casket is a weapon that once belonged to Laufey. It projects freezing blasts and can send an entire realm into an ice age. Loki tries to freeze the Bifrost in its active state, thereby destroying Jotunheim.

# HOW DOES THOR STOP HIS WICKED SIBLING?

Thor goes to drastic measures, using his hammer to smash the Bifrost bridge and collapse the entire gateway into a wormhole. Odin awakens and tries to save his sons from falling into the void but an embittered Loki lets go and falls into space. Without the bridge, poor Thor can't travel back to Earth!

**Jane** and Thor have a romantic campfire moment while discussing the cosmos and the Nine Realms.

**Heimdall** uses a sword to open and close the Bifrost—and he can see and hear everything in the Nine Realms!

The powerful **Casket of Ancient Winters** really does bring out the worst in people, as Loki discovers.

# MARVEL'S
## THE AVENGERS

**AT A GLANCE**

(Flashback) Loki makes deal with Chitauri

Thor arrives on Earth to free Loki

Cap, Iron Man and Thor fight over Loki

Tesseract activates, opening wormhole

Iron Man, Cap, and Black Widow capture Loki

Loki imprisoned on S.H.I.E.L.D.'s Helicarrier

!#*@?#!

Avengers squabble!

Loki arrives through wormhole on Earth, fights S.H.I.E.L.D.

Black Widow recruits Bruce Banner

Bruce transforms into Hulk

Hawkeye attacks Helicarrier

Nick Fury begins to enlist Avengers

Loki enslaves Hawkeye and Dr. Selvig

Black Widow breaks Loki's spell over Hawkeye

Loki opens wormhole above Stark Tower in New York

Chitauri army pours through wormhole

The Avengers assemble!

Iron Man tries to reason with Loki

Dr. Selvig reveals scepter can close the wormhole

Angry Hulk takes on Loki

Nick Fury rallies Avengers

U.N. launch nuclear missile at Manhattan

Iron Man destroys Chitauri mothership using missile

Black Widow closes wormhole

Hulk falls through sky to ground, turning back into Bruce

Thor takes defeated Loki and Tesseract to Asgard for safekeeping

Iron Man falls from sky, but Hulk catches him

Loki escapes and kills Agent Coulson

Fury promises Avengers will return

Avengers eat shawarma together

# MARVEL'S THE AVENGERS

## AN OVERVIEW

*Arriving in 2012,* Marvel's The Avengers united all of the previous Super Heroes in the MCU—Iron Man, Captain America, Thor, Hulk, Black Widow, and Hawkeye— in a single team. It also introduced actor Mark Ruffalo as Bruce Banner (Hulk).

### UNEXPECTED ARRIVAL

The creepy alien Other tells his boss, Thanos, that the Tesseract is on Earth. Loki has agreed to get it for Thanos, but he wants help conquering Earth. On Earth, Dr. Selvig is studying the Tesseract in a S.H.I.E.L.D. lab. Suddenly, it creates a portal and Loki arrives. He uses his scepter to brainwash Selvig and Hawkeye. Loki and his new minions escape with the Tesseract just before the entire facility blows up.

### SUPER HERO SELECTION

S.H.I.E.L.D. Director Nick Fury orders his agents to set up a Super Hero team. Agent Phil Coulson sends Black Widow to recruit Bruce Banner, who is currently in hiding in India where he is working as a doctor. Fury personally requests Captain America's assistance, and Coulson also asks for Tony Stark's help. Meanwhile, Loki and his entourage travel to Germany.

### APPREHENDING AN ASGARDIAN

Cap, Black Widow, and Bruce assemble on S.H.I.E.L.D.'s Helicarrier. In Germany, Loki creates a distraction so that Hawkeye can covertly steal some iridium, which they need to open a huge portal. Cap and Black Widow turn up and fight Loki, who only surrenders when Iron Man arrives and blasts him. On the way back to the Helicarrier, Thor steals Loki away, but fails to convince him to abandon his scheme. Thor eventually agrees to give Loki to S.H.I.E.L.D.

Captain America's super-human strength is still no match for an Asgardian.

### HELL ON THE HELICARRIER

Loki is imprisoned on the Helicarrier. Thor reveals Loki's plan, and Bruce and Tony realize why Loki needs iridium. The heroes bicker amongst themselves, just as Hawkeye attacks the ship. Banner transforms into Hulk during the ensuing mayhem. Loki escapes his cell, kills Coulson, and jettisons his brother. The assault renders the Helicarrier useless, but luckily the heroes free Hawkeye from Loki's mind control.

> "The Avengers. It's what we call ourselves, sort of like a team. 'Earth's Mightiest Heroes' type of thing." TONY STARK

## MAYHEM IN MANHATTAN

Loki and Selvig set up equipment to open a large portal above Stark Tower in New York City. Iron Man arrives and tries to stop them. However, the portal opens, allowing an alien army of Chitauri to invade Earth. The other Avengers turn up and battle the alien soldiers and their flying cyborg Leviathan monsters, leaving downtown New York City in a mess.

The Chitauri fly through New York City on their chariots causing chaos.

## PORTAL PINCH-OFF

Fearing a Chitauri victory, the World Security Council launches a nuclear missile at New York. Selvig—now released from Loki's magic—and Black Widow work on closing the portal, while Iron Man catches the nuclear missile and delivers it through the portal toward the Chitauri mothership on the other side. The ship is destroyed, which wipes out the Chitauri on Earth. Iron Man falls back through the portal to Earth just before Black Widow closes it. Tony's suit is powerless, so he falls toward the ground but is caught by Hulk. Loki is defeated, and Thor takes him and the Tesseract back to Asgard for safekeeping. The Avengers go their separate ways, with Nick Fury believing their victory sends a strong message to other would-be alien invaders.

Iron Man blasts the Chitauri invaders as they swarm through the portal to Earth.

# GOOD GUYS

**THE AVENGERS**
Likeable heroes,
unlikely allies

**NICK FURY**
Keeps an eye on the
Avengers

**AGENT PHIL COULSON**
Faithful to the end...
of a spear

**DR. ERIK SELVIG**
Nutty scientist,
spellbound minion

# BAD GUYS

**LOKI**
Greasy trickster with
a curvy crown

**THE OTHER**
Thanos' mouthy
mouthpiece, Loki's
liaison

**CHITAURI SOLDIERS**
With faces only the
Other could love

**THANOS**
Invisible Titan, purple
puppet-master

*Somebody must be managing all these conspicuous heroes...*

# WHAT IS S.H.I.E.L.D.?

*I've heard the name S.H.I.E.L.D. thrown around a lot. Seems like some kind of organization with a cool eagle logo.*

**S.H.I.E.L.D. LOGO**
Minimalist eagle chic

## IS IT A GEEKY FAN CLUB FOR CAPTAIN AMERICA'S SHIELD?

Sadly not! S.H.I.E.L.D. stands for the not-so-catchy "Strategic Homeland Intervention Enforcement and Logistics Division." This intelligence agency creates the Avengers Initiative to form a team of Super Heroes, with the aim of combating extraterrestrial threats.

## WHO FOUNDED IT?

S.H.I.E.L.D. was started by Howard Stark and Peggy Carter (both former S.S.R. agents), soon after World War II. At first, the agency operated in secrecy, but nowadays its existence and activities are increasingly visible to the public.

## WHO IS S.H.I.E.L.D.'s BIG CHEESE?

Nicholas "Nick" Joseph Fury is the director and primary liaison to the Avengers. He's the guy with a patch over his left eye, and the face of the organization as far as the audience is concerned. Fury must answer to the U.S. Congress, the Secretary of Defense, and the World Security Council. Despite this, sometimes S.H.I.E.L.D. does make a mess of things.

Nick Fury

# HOW DOES IT MESS UP?

S.H.I.E.L.D. tries to reactivate the Tesseract (as Red Skull did) to make weapons—not their best idea. Unfortunately, it activates spontaneously and opens a wormhole, through which Loki appears. He takes control of Selvig and Hawkeye's minds and swipes the Tesseract. Loki is later captured but escapes (he's like Houdini), resulting in an important S.H.I.E.L.D. agent's death.

**DESPERATE TIMES**
Fury takes the Tesseract and tries to make a sneaky exit before the newly-arrived Loki can get his hands on it—but to no avail.

# WHAT'S SO IMPORTANT ABOUT THIS AGENT?

Agent Phil Coulson rocks a pair of shades like no one else. He is also a loyal friend to all the Avengers. Coulson is an ally to Tony throughout his career as Iron Man, and also manages the team that finds Thor's hammer. Coulson bravely gives his life in an effort to stop Loki. Fury uses Coulson's death as inspiration to keep the Avengers together when they'd rather split apart.

**CAP'S BIGGEST FAN**
Coulson is a diehard Captain America fanboy and is super excited at the idea of Steve signing his vintage Captain America trading cards.

# MORE KEY S.H.I.E.L.D. AGENTS

**MARIA HILL**
S.H.I.E.L.D.'s deputy director. Later hired by Stark Industries but maintains close ties with Fury.

**NATASHA ROMANOFF**
Expert martial artist and former KGB assassin. Codename: Black Widow.

**SHARON CARTER**
Peggy Carter's niece. Undercover neighbor of Steve Rogers. Later joins CIA. Codename: Agent 13.

**BROCK RUMLOW**
Hydra double agent. Leader of STRIKE team, but betrays Cap. Becomes mercenary Crossbones.

**CLINT BARTON**
Best known for bow skills. Ordered to kill Black Widow but recruited her instead. Codename: Hawkeye.

He seems like such a nice, articulate, intelligent guy, so...

# WHY DOES BRUCE TURN INTO THE HULK?

*That big green thing smashes everything like a wrecking ball. Why would the Avengers want somebody like that on the team? Are they crazy?!*

## HOW DID BRUCE BECOME THE HULK?

In *The Incredible Hulk* (2008), scientist Bruce Banner underwent an experiment using gamma radiation. Although he believed it was a treatment to increase gamma resistance, the U.S. army was actually trying to create Super-Soldiers. The experiment went wrong, and as a result, Bruce now transforms into a monster called the Hulk whenever he gets angry. The Hulk state is only temporary, but he won't revert to his human form until he calms down.

The Hulk

## WHY IS BLACK WIDOW LOOKING FOR HIM?

After Loki steals the Tesseract, S.H.I.E.L.D. sends Black Widow to speak to Bruce—they need his help to track the gamma radiation it emits, so they can find Loki. As the world's foremost expert on gamma radiation, Bruce is the best man for the job! Bruce is wary of the whole thing though—he's freaked out by the thought of becoming the mega grouchy Hulk again.

# SO IS THE HULK A GOOD GUY OR A BAD ONE?

It's tricky. Bruce and the Hulk both become vital members of the Avengers thanks to Bruce's brains and the Hulk's brawn. The Avengers wouldn't have won the Battle of New York without using the Hulk's muscle against the Chitauri army. However, the Hulk is also a liability. His fiery temper tantrums can cause immense damage—a fact that Loki takes advantage of...

# THAT SOUNDS OMINOUS. WHAT'S HE UP TO NOW?

When Loki is imprisoned on the Helicarrier, he schemes to turn the Avengers against each other and enrage the Hulk, causing enough distraction and damage for Hawkeye to break Loki out. Unfortunately for the Avengers, his plan works, resulting in the Hulk raging around the Helicarrier like a bull in a china shop.

Black Widow finds Bruce living in Kolkata, India. He likes helping people, so works as a **doctor** and hasn't gone green in ages.

During the Battle of New York, Hulk happily follows Captain America's order to **"smash"** the invading Chitauri forces.

*"That's my secret, Captain: I'm always angry."* BRUCE BANNER

## CAN ANYTHING STOP THE HULK?!

Yes! Falling from a height and being knocked out reverts him into Bruce. In the later *Age of Ultron* movie, Natasha uses a calming technique to lull him back to being human. Also, Tony has a contingency plan if the Hulk can't be stopped—the Hulkbuster armor.

# BATTLE OF NEW YORK
## MADE SIMPLE

*Everything Loki's done since leaving Asgard culminates in the Chitauri invasion. The Avengers must work as a team for the first time to stop it!*

**VS.**

## WHY ARE THEY FIGHTING?

Loki opens a portal that allows the Chitauri army to invade Earth—threatening not only to destroy New York, but enslave the entire human race!

\* HELICARRIER WATCHES FROM AFAR

## INFO BOX

**COMMANDERS**—Captain America (Avengers) and Loki

**TERRAIN**—Urban landscape of New York City

**KEY BATTLE ZONES**—Stark Tower, Downtown Manhattan, the sky

## WHO IS FIGHTING WHOM

**The Avengers**

**S.H.I.E.L.D.**

**Quinjet**

**NYPD**

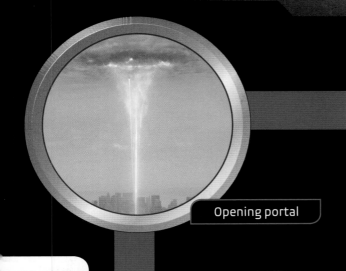

Opening portal

## KEY MOMENT

**THE HUMBLING OF LOKI**—Loki calls himself a god, but when Hulk smashes him into the floor five times, it incapacitates him! In the future he will take great pleasure seeing Hulk do the same to his brother, Thor.

Loki

Chitauri

Leviathan

Chitauri mothership

## WHO WINS?

The Avengers win and Loki loses. The Chitauri army is wiped out. However, the battle leaves human casualties in New York City, and a lot of expensive damage. Also, the experience will take a heavy toll on Tony Stark, ultimately leading to Ultron's creation.

> "That man has no regard for lawn maintenance."
>
> *TONY STARK ON THOR*

# PHASE TWO

## IRON MAN 3

**60**

### THE ONE WHERE...

Tony is back to face a brand new bad guy. This villain makes people explode, and he steals the U.S. president. Luckily, Iron Man and his partner, Pepper, save the day!

## THOR:
THE DARK WORLD

**66**

# THE ONE WHERE...
Thor takes his girlfriend, Jane, home to meet the parents, but evil, sleeping elves wake up and attack Asgard. Thor teams up with his tricksy brother, Loki, to stop them.

## CAPTAIN AMERICA:
THE WINTER SOLDIER

**72**

# THE ONE WHERE...
Cap's old pal Bucky turns up alive, but he has a weird metal arm and is shooting everyone. Cap's employer, S.H.I.E.L.D., goes bad too! Cap has a lot to sort out.

## GUARDIANS OF THE GALAXY

**78**

# THE ONE WHERE...
A heavily-tattooed alien, a green alien, a monosyllabic tree, a talking raccoon, and an Earthling walk into a bar. Then, they guard the galaxy from two other bad, blue aliens.

## AVENGERS:
AGE OF ULTRON

**84**

# THE ONE WHERE...
Tony wants a break, so creates an A.I. to avenge things instead. Shockingly, it turns evil and there's a really big battle. The good guys win, but a new hero bites the dust.

## ANT-MAN

**94**

# THE ONE WHERE...
Scott Lang gets out of jail and wants to change his life, so he steals a suit that makes him ant-sized and starts talking to ants. He fights a copycat bad guy.

# IRON MAN 3

## AN OVERVIEW

*The most recent film in the Iron Man trilogy arrived in 2013. Mainly set in 2012, the movie introduced two new charismatic villains: Aldrich Killian (played by Guy Pierce) and Trevor Slattery (by Ben Kingsley).*

### PARTY TIME

Tony Stark attends a wild New Year's Eve party in Bern, Switzerland, in 1999. He meets Maya Hansen, creator of an experimental serum named Extremis. Tony also meets and brushes off Aldrich Killian, founder of Advanced Idea Mechanics (A.I.M.).

### HAPPY NOT HAPPY

In 2012, a terrorist known as the Mandarin claims responsibility for bombings across the U.S. Meanwhile, Tony is having anxiety attacks about the Battle of New York. Pepper Potts has a meeting with Killian, who is now a rich CEO. Killian shows off the healing capabilities of Extremis. Soon after, a man explodes in Grauman's Chinese Theatre, sending Tony's friend Happy Hogan to hospital and killing some civilians. Oddly, Killian's bodyguard, Savin, is caught in the blast but walks away, casually regenerating a lost limb. Tony issues a televised challenge to fight the Mandarin.

> **"A famous man once said, 'We create our own demons.'"**
>
> *TONY STARK*

### BRINGING THE HOUSE DOWN

Back at his Malibu mansion, Tony studies the attacks, deducing that the first bomb exploded in Tennessee. Maya turns up at the mansion, but it is suddenly attacked by armed helicopters and turned to rubble. While Pepper and Maya escape, Tony sinks into the sea wearing an Iron Man suit, and is presumed dead. Maya reveals to Pepper that she thinks Killian works for the Mandarin.

**Attack helicopters completely demolish Tony Stark's Malibu home.**

### FLEE TO TENNESSEE

Tony's A.I., JARVIS, takes over the suit to save an unconscious Tony from drowning. He wakes up as the suit crashes into snow in Tennessee, the last location programmed into the suit. Lacking enough power to return home, Tony meets a boy named Harley who helps him out. Just as Tony receives key details on Extremis from a local, he is attacked by Killian's agents, but defeats them. He then illegally accesses A.I.M.'s database, and discovers the bombs were actually injured veterans who were given Extremis, but couldn't adapt to it, and blew up.

## TROUBLE WITH TREVOR

Maya turns against Pepper and helps Killian kidnap her, and one of his agents also traps Rhodey. Meanwhile, Tony traces the Mandarin to a Miami compound, and discovers the villain is actually an actor named Trevor Slattery. Then, Killian captures Tony, and reveals he is the brains behind the operation. Killian gives Pepper Extremis to force Tony into fixing the explosive side-effects. Suddenly, Maya develops a conscience, so Killian murders her.

## ATTACK ON AIR FORCE ONE

Killian uses his Extremis powers to force Rhodey out of his suit, and tells him that he wants to kidnap President Ellis. Savin uses Rhodey's suit to attack Air Force One, and puts Ellis in the suit. Tony and Rhodey escape the Miami compound, and manage to kill Savin. However, they cannot rescue Ellis, as the suit, flying on autopilot, takes him to Killian's location.

## KILLING KILLIAN

Tony and Rhodey trace Killian to an oil tanker where he plans to kill Ellis live on television. Tony summons all of his Iron Man suits to operate as drones and help their rescue mission. While Rhodey saves Ellis, Tony tries to save Pepper, but she seems to fall to a fiery death. Killian appears invincible as Tony fights him, even surviving confinement in an exploding suit. Thanks to Extremis, Pepper emerges from the flames unharmed and defeats Killian.

Iron Man and an Extremis-powered Aldrich Killian fight to the death aboard an oil tanker.

## AFTERMATH

As proof of his love for Pepper, Tony creates a fireworks display by exploding all of his Iron Man suits. Trevor is arrested. Pepper is cured of Extremis, and Tony has the shrapnel in his chest removed.

# GOOD GUYS

**IRON MAN (TONY STARK)**
Stressed-out hero, far from home

**IRON PATRIOT (RHODEY RHODES)**
Same armored friend, rebranded

**PEPPER POTTS**
CEO turned Extremis-powered fighter

**HAPPY HOGAN**
Slightly-charred chief of security

# BAD GUYS

**ALDRICH KILLIAN**
Master behind the "Mandarin"

**TREVOR SLATTERY**
The fake Mandarin, attention-seeking actor

**ERIC SAVIN**
Hot-headed henchman, president kidnapper

**MAYA HANSEN**
Noble scientific aspirations gone wrong

*Poor Tony seems to have a lot on his plate...*

# WHAT IS THE NEW DANGER?

*I know there's lots of explosions and there's a villain sporting a trendy beard and a man-bun. But why is Tony struggling to deal with things these days?*

**JUST CHILLING**
Tony had a long flight

## WHAT'S THE TROUBLE NOW?

Bombings around the U.S. are causing widespread panic. It appears that terrorists are acting as suicide bombers, but they aren't leaving any evidence behind. Tony's friend and Stark Industries Chief of Security Harold "Happy" Hogan is gravely injured in one of these attacks.

## WHO IS DOING THIS?

A mysterious bearded figure calling himself the Mandarin claims to be behind the bombings. He appears to be the leader of The Ten Rings—the same terrorist organization that kidnapped Tony in the first *Iron Man* movie. Tony has a tough time dealing with this, especially with new problems of his own.

> *"You know who I am. You don't know where I am. And you'll NEVER see me coming."*
>
> *THE MANDARIN*

# OH, NO. WHAT KIND OF PROBLEMS?

Tony is suffering from anxiety attacks after his experiences during the Battle of New York, and specifically the trauma of flying into a Chitauri wormhole, before falling back to Earth. He can't sleep, so is tinkering on his suits constantly, and he's afraid of losing his girlfriend, Pepper Potts.

# HOW DOES TONY DEAL WITH THE MANDARIN?

Tony issues a challenge to the Mandarin, but the response is more than he can handle. His home is obliterated by attack helicopters! With help from JARVIS, Tony escapes in his new Mark XLII suit (he has a lot of suits now), but it is damaged and low on power, leaving Tony stranded and alone—in a large amount of snow—trying to find the elusive Mandarin.

# DOES TONY FIND HIM?

Tony tracks down the Mandarin, but he's not hiding in some overseas Ten Rings base like Tony expected. He's in Miami! There, Tony discovers the Mandarin is actually a professional actor named Trevor Slattery. This inebriated imposter is a bumbling fool, manufactured to be a distraction from the real menace—and the true source of the explosions!

After the Battle of New York, Pepper and Tony have started **living together**, but things can get a bit tense at times.

When his Iron Man **suit is damaged**, Tony has to rely on a more dated method of communication than he is used to.

Tony befriends **Harley** in Tennessee. This resourceful child helps Tony repair his broken suit and investigate the bombing.

# WHY ARE PEOPLE EXPLODING?

*At first they seemed like terrorists, but the Mandarin's molten minions look like they have super-powers they can't control. What's going on here?*

## WHEN DID THESE PYROTECHNIC PROBLEMS ALL BEGIN?

A scientist named Maya Hansen invented a treatment called Extremis as a way to help people recover from injuries. Unfortunately, Extremis has a nasty habit of making some of its recipients explode. Maya showed Tony her research back in 1999, but he wasn't interested because of the undesirable side effects. This left Maya to look for another financial backer.

## SO WHO IS DEVELOPING EXTREMIS NOW?

A rival company of Stark Industries called Advanced Idea Mechanics (A.I.M.) recruited Maya to develop her research. The company is owned by Aldrich Killian, who used Extremis on himself. He also tested it on willing test subjects, but couldn't fix the flaw...

**TESTING TRIAL**
Ellen Brandt successfully adapts to Extremis. She loyally serves Killian and starts a barroom brawl with Tony.

## WHAT EXACTLY HAPPENS TO THE TEST SUBJECTS?

Wounded military veterans volunteer for Extremis trials. Most of them gain super-strength and agility, as well as the incredible ability to heal deep wounds, even regenerating lost limbs. Their bodies can also generate ridiculously high temperatures. Killian can even breathe fire! However, some people just can't handle the heat and blow up.

# WHAT IS KILLIAN'S MASTER PLAN?

After fabricating the Mandarin, Killian wants to control the presidency too. Then, he can oversee both sides of the war on terror. Killian plans to kill the current president, and replace him with someone he can boss around. That someone is the vice president, whom Killian has recruited by offering to give his daughter Extremis.

# HOW DOES IRON MAN STOP KILLIAN?

Tony and Rhodey track down Killian, who has also kidnapped Pepper Potts and infected her with Extremis. Tony summons his many new Iron Man suits (which function as autonomous robots) to help him, but it is the Extremis-powered Pepper who kills the nearly indestructible Killian.

## WAIT, SO WAS KILLIAN THE REAL MANDARIN?

As we know, Trevor Slattery actually worked for Aldrich Killian, who was the man behind the Mandarin—the fake leader of The Ten Rings terrorist group. However, The Ten Rings isn't a fake organization (they captured Tony in the first film). It remains to be seen if there is a real leader of this shadowy group...

After the president is nearly killed in the Iron Patriot suit, Rhodey returns to using his **War Machine** codename.

Tony has built many suits of armor. Some are specialized suits, like the **Mark XXXVII**, which excels underwater.

**Pepper** mixes Tony's technology and her Extremis-induced powers to take down Killian once and for all.

# THOR: THE DARK WORLD

*The second movie in the* Thor *saga arrived in 2013. Directed by Alan Taylor,* Thor: The Dark World *saw the return of the previous film's principal characters, but also the death of Thor's mother Frigga, played by actress Rene Russo.*

## HIBERNATING ELVES

In ancient times, Bor—Odin's dad—battled the sinister leader of the Dark Elves, Malekith, and his forces on Svartalfheim. Just before Malekith could unleash his super weapon (known as the Aether) upon the universe, Bor stole it away. Bor thought he had wiped out the Dark Elves, but Malekith and a small group escaped and went into hibernation, awaiting the next Convergence, when the Nine Realms would align once more and he could try again. Legends said Bor destroyed the Aether, but they were false. Instead he hid it away deep below the surface of Svartalfheim. But maybe not deep enough...

## JANE MEETS THE AETHER

On Earth, Jane Foster accidentally passes through one of these portals, where she discovers the hidden Aether trapped in a column of stone. Jane becomes infected by the Aether and Thor's friend Heimdall alerts him that she has passed out of his all-seeing cosmic vision. Thor rushes to Earth and finds Jane overcome by the supernatural force.

## A TRIP TO THE DOCTOR

Thor brings Jane to Asgard, hoping the doctors there can cure her ailment. They discover that she is carrying the Aether, which not only threatens to kill her, but also to bring about the end of the universe. Malekith senses the Aether's return and invades Asgard. His lieutenant Algrim kills Frigga, who was protecting Jane. Malekith is then driven from Asgard empty-handed.

## RESTORING THE NINE REALMS

In the present day, the Bifrost bridge has been rebuilt (since its destruction in *Thor*) and Asgardians can visit the other realms once more. Thor and his friends restore order in the realms after their long absence, culminating in a battle on Vanaheim. Meanwhile, Loki is imprisoned on Asgard for his crimes during the Battle of New York (seen in *Marvel's: The Avengers*). All seems right in the realms again, but a new Convergence of the Nine Reams is about to occur, waking Malekith from his long slumber and opening portals between the nine worlds.

Malekith's ship crashes into the throne room of the Royal Palace on Asgard. Very inconsiderate of him!

## "I better get my pants."

*ERIK SELVIG*

## GOOD GUYS

**THOR**
Disobeys dad again
to save universe

**DR. JANE FOSTER**
Carrying cosmic
annihilation and a PhD

### SNEAKING OFF TO SVARTALFHEIM

Odin locks the Bifrost and forbids travel from Asgard to protect his people. Seeking to cure Jane, stop Malekith, and avenge his mother's death, Thor enlists the help of Loki to find a secret gateway from Asgard to Svartalfheim. Once on Svartalfheim, Thor and Loki hope that Malekith will draw the Aether from Jane and they may then destroy it before it bonds with the Dark Elf. The Aether proves far too virulent however. Malekith captures the weapon and departs. Loki appears to be killed in a fight with Algrim.

**LOKI**
Changes allegiance
in every scene

**FRIGGA**
Best mom in the
universe award

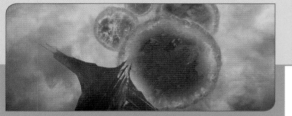

The Nine Realms converge above Greenwich, England, offering Earth a peek at alien worlds, before annihilation.

**DR. ERIK SELVIG**
Runs around
Stonehenge naked

**DARCY LEWIS**
Intern with an intern,
first-date crasher

### GREENWICH SHOWDOWN

Thor and Jane head back to Earth and enlist the help of her assistant Darcy, Darcy's intern Ian, and Dr. Selvig. Thor battles Malekith as they tumble through portals between Svartalfheim and Earth. Just as Malekith is about to plunge the universe into darkness with the Aether, Jane's team uses their scientific gear to open a portal and pull Malekith into it—preventing him from accomplishing his cataclysmic goal, and crushing him underneath his own ship. Thor returns to Asgard and tells his father he does not wish to become king. However—shocker!—Odin is actually Loki in disguise, who survived Svartalfheim. The Aether is later transferred to the safekeeping of a mysterious man, known as the Collector.

## BAD GUYS

**MALEKITH**
Half-charred elf
with a lovely braid

**ALGRIM**
Bad elf
goes badder

**67**

*Peace never lasts very long in the MCU, so...*

# WHAT THREATENS THE UNIVERSE THIS TIME?

Malekith

*Loki is off to prison and Thor is finally setting the Nine Realms back in order. Aren't things looking rosy? What's with the impending darkness?*

## WHO ARE THOR'S NEW, POINTY-EARED FOES?

The Dark Elves are Asgard's oldest adversaries. They were born just before the dawn of the universe in total darkness. Odin's father, Bor, thought he had destroyed them, but their leader Malekith and a small army retreated. They hid in suspended animation, waiting for the perfect time to return.

## WHY DO THEY COME CRAWLING BACK NOW?

Malekith awakes at the start of the Convergence—an extraordinary alignment of the Nine Realms, which opens portals between the worlds. He also senses that his lost super weapon has been found and activated. These two events are vital to execute his plan.

> *"Have you come to witness the end of your universe?"*
>
> MALEKITH TO THOR

# A PLAN, YOU SAY?

Indeed. Malekith wants to recover his creepy super weapon, known as the Aether. This crimson-and-black force appears simultaneously as a gas, liquid, and solid. It tends to dwell inside living hosts, but only the most powerful masters can wield it with success. Malekith yearns to usher in cosmic destruction by returning the universe to darkness, but his scheme hits a snag...

# WHAT'S THE FLY IN THE OINTMENT?

Dr. Jane Foster slips through a portal in London on Earth, and accidentally discovers the Aether first! She gets infected by it and is taken to Asgard by Thor, where Odin's doctors diagnose the Aether inside her. They determine it will kill her if it isn't removed. Malekith then attacks Asgard in an attempt to retrieve the Aether. However, he is foiled in the attempt and leaves without his prize.

# HOW DOES THOR TRY TO SAVE JANE?

Thor, Loki, and Jane travel to Malekith's home world, Svartalfheim. Thor and Loki trick Malekith into drawing the Aether out of Jane, thinking they can then destroy it. They fail miserably though, and Malekith departs with the Aether, bent on destruction (and maintaining his luxurious blond braid).

**INTRUDER ALERT**
Even the mighty Heimdall is horrified by the sight of Malekith's enormous Ark warship looming ominously over Asgard.

Malekith's ship smashes into Greenwich. Dark Elves aren't big on considerate parking.

# HOW DO THOR AND THE GANG STOP HIM?

Malekith travels to Greenwich, London, and unleashes the Aether during the Convergence. After a tense battle, Jane's team and Thor use experimental equipment to transport Malekith back to Svartalfheim in several gruesome pieces. His ship follows swiftly behind through a portal, and squashes him flat. Poor Malekith never gets to carry out his glorious intergalactic annihilation!

He looks rather greasy and I'm not sure I'd trust him...

# IS LOKI EVIL?

Loki is back again and at the center of calamity, as always. At times he can be quite charming... does he have any redeeming qualities? Or is he as bad as his hair suggests?

**FRIGGA**
Mother of gods...

## WHY IS LOKI IN CHAINS?

After the Battle of New York, Thor takes Loki back to Asgard to stand trial for his evil deeds. It's safe to say that Odin is less than impressed with Loki, and hasn't failed to notice that war, ruin, and death follow Loki around like a magnet.

## WHAT ARE LOKI'S POWERS?

Loki uses magic to project illusions. He can disguise himself as other people, or even cast doppelgängers, using the duplicates to see and communicate remotely. Loki learned his magic skills from his mother, Frigga. It's a shame she didn't teach him to wash his hair more often, but you can't have everything.

## WHY IS HE SUCH A JERK?

Loki was always jealous of his older brother, feeling Thor was neither intelligent nor noble enough to rule. Loki resents that Odin is disapproving of him, while favoring Thor. Loki thinks Odin scorns him because Loki is an alien (he discovered his real dad is Laufey the Frost Giant in *Thor*, remember?), rather than admitting his own devious actions are the problem.

Loki

# SO MUCH DRAMA! DOES LOKI HATE HIS FAMILY?

Yes and no. Loki is understandably bitter about being lied to his whole life and strikes out at his father. Yet when his mother dies, he mourns her. He may betray Thor and Odin over and over again, but he retains a bond with them. Loki and Thor also put their differences aside to avenge their mother's murder and save Jane and the Nine Realms.

# SO LOKI ISN'T ALL BAD?

Loki is known as the god of mischief, but he's not merely a trickster. He has done lots of terrible things, too—like trying to conquer Earth and killing lots of innocent people! Loki does seem to have a little good in him, though. He's willing to help Thor, even if it means giving up his own life.

# DOES HE DIE THIS TIME?

Nope. There's always a catch to these things when Loki is involved! Loki appears to die while saving Thor from Malekith's lieutenant, Algrim. His death is in fact an illusion, and Loki secretly returns to Asgard to usurp his father.

# DOES HE KILL HIS FATHER?

Loki masquerades as Odin, but his father isn't dead. Loki doesn't actually hate Odin enough to kill him. As we discover in *Thor: Ragnarok*, he merely places him under a spell and enrolls him in the Shady Acres retirement home on Earth! Sounds delightful...

Odin imprisons Loki in the **Asgardian Dungeons** for his crimes on Earth. Loki still gets a luxurious cell, however!

Disobeying Odin yet again, Thor frees Loki and the brothers travel to a **secret portal**, sneaking Jane out of Asgard.

On gloomy Svartalflheim a bunch of unfriendly **Dark Elves** circle Loki, but he doesn't waste any time flattening them.

# CAPTAIN AMERICA:
## THE WINTER SOLDIER

## AN OVERVIEW

*The Winter Soldier* was the second *Captain America* movie, *premiering in 2014. Actor Sebastian Stan returned as Bucky, now with a sinister Winter Soldier alter ego. The film introduced a new future Avenger: Falcon, played by Anthony Mackie.*

### RESCUE MISSION

Steve Rogers now lives in Washington, D.C. as a S.H.I.E.L.D. employee. He finds it hard adapting to modern life, but makes friends with veteran Sam Wilson. Steve, Natasha Romanoff, and Agent Brock Rumlow go on a mission to rescue some agents held hostage on a hijacked S.H.I.E.L.D. ship. Steve sees Natasha splitting off with separate secret orders to copy the vessel's data—and wants to know why.

### FURY IN JEOPARDY

Later, in his car, Fury is ambushed by assassins and nearly killed by an agent known as the Winter Soldier. Fury makes it to Steve's apartment and gives him a flash drive with the S.H.I.E.L.D. data from the ship. In the process he is gunned down by the Winter Soldier and pronounced dead in surgery.

The Winter Soldier ruthlessly pursues Nick Fury through the streets of Washington D.C.

### PROJECT INSIGHT

Back at S.H.I.E.L.D. HQ, Steve questions Nick Fury about the mission. Fury debriefs him on Project Insight: Three new Helicarriers are being built, linked to spy satellites programed to monitor the world and identify emerging threats. Later, Fury becomes troubled when he is locked out of the S.H.I.E.L.D. data recovered by Natasha. He asks Defense Secretary Alexander Pierce to delay Project Insight but is rebuffed.

### CAP ON THE RUN

Before he died, Fury told Steve to trust no one, so Steve withholds information about events from Secretary Pierce. Pierce brands Steve a traitor and sends a team led by Rumlow to kill him. He escapes and enlists the help of Natasha. They use the flash drive data to locate a secret bunker at Steve's old military training base.

> ## "S.H.I.E.L.D. takes the world as it is, not as we'd like it to be."
> *NICK FURY TO STEVE ROGERS*

### THE UGLY TRUTH

Below the bunker, the heroes find an outdated supercomputer that contains the consciousness of Arnim Zola (last seen in the first *Captain America* movie). He reveals that Hydra has corrupted S.H.I.E.L.D. from within, manipulating the public to give up their freedom in exchange for security. Then, a S.H.I.E.L.D. missile destroys the bunker, but the heroes take cover under Cap's shield.

### FALCON ON BOARD

Steve and Natasha ask Sam Wilson for help. Sam acquires his old experimental Falcon wingpack and helps them capture S.H.I.E.L.D. agent Jasper Sitwell, who reveals Project Insight's true purpose: To eliminate anyone who could pose a threat to Hydra. The Winter Soldier interrupts and kills Sitwell. The heroes chase the Winter Soldier, but Steve recognizes him as his old friend Bucky, now a brainwashed Hydra assassin. Agent Hill catches up with Steve, Natasha, and Sam, taking them to see Fury, who it turns out had faked his death.

### THE END OF S.H.I.E.L.D.?

S.H.I.E.L.D. initiates its plan and launches the Helicarriers. Fury and Natasha infiltrate S.H.I.E.L.D. HQ, take out Pierce, and broadcast all of Hydra and S.H.I.E.L.D.'s secrets over the internet. Meanwhile, Steve and Sam board the Helicarriers and replace their control chips, allowing Hill to destroy them remotely. The events culminate in a showdown between Cap and the Winter Soldier. They crash into the Potomac River, but the Winter Soldier pulls Steve to shore, saving his life, and then vanishes.

A Helicarrier crashes into S.H.I.E.L.D. headquarters (known as the Triskelion), and demolishes the entire building.

## GOOD GUYS

**CAPTAIN AMERICA
(STEVE ROGERS)**
All-American hero with
a few good friends

**BLACK WIDOW
(NATASHA ROMANOFF)**
S.H.I.E.L.D. agent,
leaker of secrets

**FALCON
(SAM WILSON)**
Cap's new flighted
friend

**NICK FURY**
Caught in a Hydra
blind spot

## BAD GUYS

**WINTER SOLDIER
(BUCKY BARNES)**
Shiny-armed assassin

**JASPER SITWELL**
Background good
guy, now bad

**BROCK RUMLOW**
Hydra/S.H.I.E.L.D.
double-agent

There's a new guy with a mask and a silver arm...

# WHO IS THE WINTER SOLDIER?

So the Winter Soldier runs around shooting things and blowing up stuff—but is he another hero or a new villain?

**BUCKY BARNES**
Wartime warrior

## HAVE I MET HIM BEFORE?

Yes! The Winter Soldier is actually Captain America's friend Bucky Barnes, who served with him in World War II (last seen in *Captain America: The First Avenger*). He works for Hydra now, though clearly he also has been involved with the Soviets—his most distinguishing feature is a bionic arm decorated with a red Soviet star.

## I THOUGHT BUCKY DIED?

So did Captain America! Bucky fell from a Hydra train in 1945 during a mission to capture Dr. Arnim Zola (Red Skull's sidekick). He was found, badly wounded, by Soviet soldiers and handed over to Hydra. Between missions for Hydra, Bucky was placed in cryogenic hibernation to stall his aging.

## IS HE BRAINWASHED?

Yes, indeed! Dr. Zola subjected Bucky to a rigorous and painful program to wipe his mind clean. If the Winter Soldier shows any signs of resistance or lack of clarity, his mind is wiped and reprogramed all over again. However, the reprograming isn't entirely effective...

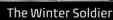

The Winter Soldier

# DOES HE REMEMBER STEVE ROGERS?

Not at first. When he fights Captain America, the Winter Soldier's mask is accidentally torn off. Cap recognizes him and calls out Bucky's name. Though it's not instantaneous, Bucky's memories are triggered. Unfortunately Hydra simply wipes his mind again. In his final clash with Steve Rogers, Bucky begins to remember again and saves Cap from drowning—before vanishing.

Hydra conducted **horrific experiments** on Bucky, turning him into a weapon.

# SO THE WINTER SOLDIER ISN'T EVIL?

As the Winter Soldier, Bucky Barnes has done a lot of terrible things in the service of Hydra. He has assassinated lots of people, and even shot (though not fatally) Black Widow, Nick Fury, and Captain America! Some of his worst deeds are yet to be uncovered. None of these things were done in his right mind, however. Zola has not won—the hero Bucky is still inside.

The Winter Soldier's **bionic arm** gives him super-human strength.

# HOW DID ZOLA END UP IN THE MIDDLE OF THIS?

After Dr. Zola was captured in WWII, he was recruited by S.H.I.E.L.D., but continued to operate as a Hydra double-agent. During this time he sought to make the Winter Soldier the new "fist of Hydra." When his body died in 1972, Zola's mind was transferred to a super-computer, where he carried out Hydra's plans from beyond the grave.

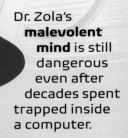

Dr. Zola's **malevolent mind** is still dangerous even after decades spent trapped inside a computer.

_I thought Captain America was the country's biggest hero..._

# SO WHY IS CAP ON THE RUN?

**FALCON**
Sam Wilson with wings

_Captain America is a member of the Avengers and now works for S.H.I.E.L.D., but currently he isn't very popular with his colleagues. Why are they after him?_

## HOW IS CAP ADJUSTING TO 21ST-CENTURY LIFE?

Steve is still getting used to it. Many of the people he once knew are dead. There are positives, however, such as surfing the internet and catching up on awesome music that he missed. Fortunately he makes a new friend— Sam Wilson, an Air Force veteran working at the VA (Veterans Affairs). Steve also works with Natasha at S.H.I.E.L.D., but his work life isn't exactly great at the moment.

## WHO IS AFTER CAP?

S.H.I.E.L.D.—or rather, Hydra posing as S.H.I.E.L.D.! After WWII, S.H.I.E.L.D. recruited Hydra agent Dr. Arnim Zola for his scientific expertise, but he used the organization's resources to secretly rebuild Hydra from within. Hydra's infiltration spans every level, up to and including Secretary of Defense Alexander Pierce!

**WARRIORS' BOND**
Steve and Sam first meet when Steve repeatedly (and somewhat annoyingly) laps Sam on his morning run.

**NEED-TO-KNOW**
Tensions between Steve and Natasha rise when he suspects that she is keeping things from him.

# SO WHAT'S HYDRA'S NEW SCHEME?

Pierce oversees a new program called Project Insight. The venture features three advanced Helicarriers that permanently remain in flight, linked to orbiting spy satellites. The diabolical aspect of the program employs a secret algorithm developed by Zola, which scans all of Earth's digital records and locates potential future threats to Hydra. The Helicarriers will then assassinate them pre-emptively.

**NEW TOYS**
Fury takes Cap on a Project Insight tour—consisting of a secret collection of super-duper, high-tech, giant Helicarriers.

# HOW CAN HYDRA GET AWAY WITH THIS?

When Nick Fury raises concerns about Project Insight, Pierce sends the Winter Soldier to get rid of him. Fury manages to escape and warn Steve, only to be shot and seemingly killed. Steve is soon blamed for the director's murder by Pierce, and hunted by S.H.I.E.L.D. Cap would be doomed if it weren't for Natasha and Sam!

# HOW DO NATASHA, SAM, AND STEVE FOIL HYDRA?

While Natasha infiltrates the Triskelion (S.H.I.E.L.D. headquarters), Steve and Sam board the Insight Helicarriers and gain control. Sam is aided by an experimental wingpack that allows him to fly, earning him the codename "Falcon." Despite formidable interference from the Winter Soldier, the heroes are able to destroy the three Helicarriers.

**FALL OF S.H.I.E.L.D.**
In the climactic battle at the Triskelion, loyal S.H.I.E.L.D. agents must fight Hydra infiltrators who, moments before, were friends and colleagues.

# IS THIS THE END OF NICK FURY AND S.H.I.E.L.D.?

No and yes, respectively. It turns out the Winter Soldier didn't actually succeed in killing Nick Fury. Fury used the opportunity to fake his own death and then went into hiding. Natasha uploads all of S.H.I.E.L.D.'s data to the internet in order to expose Hydra, which effectively cripples both organizations. This marks the end of S.H.I.E.L.D., for now.

# GUARDIANS OF THE GALAXY

## AN OVERVIEW

*This 2014 space adventure comedy was the first in the* Guardians of the Galaxy *series.* GOTG *featured Chris Pratt in his breakout role as Peter Quill. Fans especially fell in love with two computer-generated characters: Rocket and Groot.*

### QUEST FOR THE ORB

In 1988 young Peter Quill's mother dies from a brain tumor. Outside the hospital, he is abducted by the alien Yondu Udonta and his Ravager space pirates. In the present day, the adult Peter, aka Star-Lord, steals a mysterious Orb on the planet Morag. A Kree warlord known as Ronan the Accuser is also after the Orb—his lieutenant, Korath, intercepts Peter, but he escapes in his ship. Instead of bringing the Orb to Yondu, as Peter was hired to do, he tries to sell it to a dealer on the planet Xandar. Yondu angrily issues a bounty for Peter's capture.

### FOLLIES ON XANDAR

Peter's dealer wants nothing to do with the Orb when he learns Ronan is after it. Gamora, an associate of Ronan and the adopted daughter of the "Mad Titan" Thanos, steals the Orb from Peter. As she runs, bounty hunters Rocket and Groot capture Peter. All are then apprehended by the Nova Corps (Xandar's police force).

### GOING KNOWHERE

In prison, the four meet an inmate, Drax, who seeks revenge on Ronan. Drax tries to kill Gamora due to her association with Ronan, but Peter persuades him that she is now against her former ally. All five then work together to escape, leaving the prison in chaos. The group heads to a space outpost called Knowhere in order to sell the Orb. Their buyer, the Collector, reveals that the Orb conceals an Infinity Stone: an object of limitless destructive power. The Collector's servant grabs the stone, accidentally causing a huge explosion. Gamora realizes it isn't safe to leave the Orb with the Collector, so takes it and tries to leave in a pod. However, Drax has issued a rash challenge to Ronan, whose forces arrive at Knowhere.

> **"I'm going to die surrounded by the biggest idiots in the galaxy."** *GAMORA*

Drax issues a personal challenge to Ronan that nearly gets everyone killed. Oh dear.

## YONDU SAVES THE DAY

Nebula—Gamora's evil sister and Ronan's ally—destroys Gamora's pod and leaves her floating in space. The Orb ends up in Ronan's clutches. Peter saves Gamora and, in desperation, contacts Yondu. Peter promises Yondu the Orb if Yondu will return Peter and Gamora to their ship. Peter's new friends agree they can't let Ronan use the Infinity Stone, so make a plan to go after him. Meanwhile Ronan turns against his master, Thanos, and plans to wield the stone to destroy Xandar.

## RONAN'S RUIN

Peter and his friends band together with Yondu's Ravagers and the Nova Corps to save Xandar. The Guardians (except Rocket) board Ronan's vessel, the *Dark Aster*, while the others attack from their ships. Ronan uses the Infinity Stone, now in his war hammer, to destroy the attacking fleet. Gamora fights Nebula and wins, but Nebula escapes. The Guardians appear outmatched until Rocket crashes a ship into Ronan's vessel. As the *Dark Aster* plummets, Groot sacrifices himself to shield them all. On the ground, the Guardians team up to help Peter put an end to Ronan.

**It's the Nova Corps, flying cool, star-shaped ships! These brave pilots try to protect Xandar from Ronan.**

## HEROES OF XANDAR

Peter hands over the Orb to Yondu, sneakily switching the Infinity Stone for a toy troll. Peter gives the real Infinity Stone to the Nova Corps for safekeeping. In return, the Corps delete the Guardians' criminal records. They also mention to Peter that their scans show he is only half human. As the Guardians of the Galaxy depart, Rocket clutches a freshly planted sapling of Groot.

# GOOD GUYS

**STAR-LORD (PETER QUILL)**
Loves mixtapes and rulebreaking

**GAMORA**
Wanted assassin, doesn't dance

**DRAX**
Muscleman, takes everything literally

**ROCKET AND GROOT**
A talking raccoon and a walking tree

# BAD GUYS

**RONAN**
Furious warlord with heavy hammer

**NEBULA**
Cyborg sister with daddy issues

**THANOS**
Big boss with unreliable employees

**YONDU**
Ravager pirate, likes whistling and arrows

*This is a pretty strange-looking team...*

# HOW DID THIS GANG GET TOGETHER?!

*I see a talking raccoon, a walking tree, an emerald woman, a tattooed muscleman, and a guy wearing headphones named "Star-Lord." Are they from outer space?*

**ROCKET**
A very angry critter

## IS STAR-LORD HUMAN?

Peter Quill (Star-Lord) is the only human in the Guardians team. That being said, we discover at the end of the film that he is *half* human (on his mom's side). Peter was born on Earth, but was abducted as a child by Ravager pirate Yondu Udonta, and raised off-world. His real problems begin when he meets Rocket and the other Guardians.

## SO IS ROCKET AN "EARTH RACCOON"?

So it seems! However, Rocket has been both genetically and cybernetically enhanced, and he's not only sentient—he's grouchy and selfish too! He and his business partner, Groot, end up tangled in a fight between Peter and famed assassin Gamora on the planet Xandar.

Gamora

Star-Lord

Drax the Destroyer

Rocket

## IS GAMORA A VILLAIN?

No! Gamora is Thanos' adopted daughter, but she betrays him. She tries to steal a mysterious Orb from Peter, but instead of delivering it to Thanos as ordered, she intends to sell it to the "Collector." Nonetheless, things don't go quite as planned—and new teammate Drax is partly to blame.

The Orb

## HOW DOES DRAX MESS THINGS UP?

Drax issues a rash challenge to Thanos' vicious ally, Ronan. Drax wants revenge after Ronan murdered his family. In the chaos of an accidental explosion at the Collector's museum, Ronan arrives and takes the Orb. The Guardians pursue Ronan to his ship above Xandar, where they would have all died, if not for Groot.

## HOW DOES GROOT SAVE THE DAY?

Although the only words sentient plant Groot can say are "I am Groot" (over and over again), he's actually quite kind and thoughtful. When Ronan's ship is about to crash, he grows into a protective hedge around his friends. Although he saves them, Groot is smashed to pieces. Rocket plants a cutting of him, however, and grows an adorable new baby Groot!

The creepy Kree named **Korath** is Ronan's lieutenant. He and Star-Lord battle for the Orb on the planet Morag.

**Yondu** has a complicated relationship with Peter. Although Yondu takes out a bounty on Peter, he also cares about him.

The **Kyln** is a dangerous, high-security prison, where these odd individuals are first thrown together as a team. Yay!

# WHO ARE THE GUARDIANS' FOES?

*One of them likes wearing war paint and keeps popping up like a bad smell. The other is big, purple, sits on a hovering throne in space, and doesn't get much screen time. Are they a big deal?*

## WHO'S THE GLARING GUY IN THE HOOD?

Villainous Ronan is a Kree alien with a fanatical hatred for the Xandarian people and a penchant for being daubed in creepy makeup. Furious at a peace treaty between Xandar and the Kree Empire, he's determined to have his revenge and wipe out the Xandarians.

## AND WHO'S THE GUY ON THE THRONE?

Thanos, also called "The Mad Titan." He is referred to as "the most powerful being in the universe." This smirking, sinister figure sits on a hovering techno-mystic chair and makes a deal with Ronan. Keep an eye on Thanos, he will become the MCU's biggest threat!

## WHAT IS THIS DEAL?

Thanos promises to help Ronan destroy Xandar, in exchange for Ronan retrieving the Orb and delivering it to Thanos—but Ronan keeps it for himself and tries to destroy Xandar all on his own. Ultimately Ronan disappoints Thanos, much like Gamora and Nebula.

# NEBULA? WHO'S SHE?

Nebula is a blue-skinned cyborg and another adopted daughter of Thanos (making her Gamora's sister). She sides with Ronan against her father, whom she deeply hates. Fortunately for Thanos, he has other children to aid him later... though they are yet to be revealed.

**IT'S PERSONAL!**
Ronan really, REALLY hates Xandar! After a thousand years of war, he feels the peace treaty is a betrayal of all the Kree who died in the fighting.

# WHAT IS THANOS ACTUALLY UP TO?

Thanos wants the Infinity Stones. According to the Collector, before the dawn of the universe, there existed six singularities, which were forged into stones. The Orb contains one of them, known as the Power Stone. Thanos wants to wield all six by harnessing their collective power within his "Infinity Gauntlet"—and with it, rule the universe!

# WHAT HAPPENS IF YOU TOUCH A STONE?

That depends! It helps if you're already powerful. When the Collector's servant Carina touches the Power Stone, it causes her to explode! Ronan survives brief contact with the same stone, as does Star-Lord (but only because of his Celestial DNA, and help from the other Guardians, who share the stone's power between them to destroy Ronan).

# LIST OF INFINITY STONES

**Space Stone**
Concealed in the Tesseract. It is a source of limitless energy and allows the user to travel anywhere.

**Reality Stone**
Disguised as the Aether. The stone (in liquid form) enters a being and grants the power to alter reality itself.

**Time Stone**
Powers Doctor Strange's Eye of Agamotto. It allows the wielder to bend time to their will.

**Power Stone**
Encased in the Orb. It bestows enough power to destroy entire planets, but usually kills anyone who touches it!

**Mind Stone**
Mounted in Loki's scepter; later set in Vision's forehead. It controls minds and bestows super-powers.

**Soul Stone**
Yet to be revealed.

# AVENGERS:
## AGE OF ULTRON

## AT A GLANCE

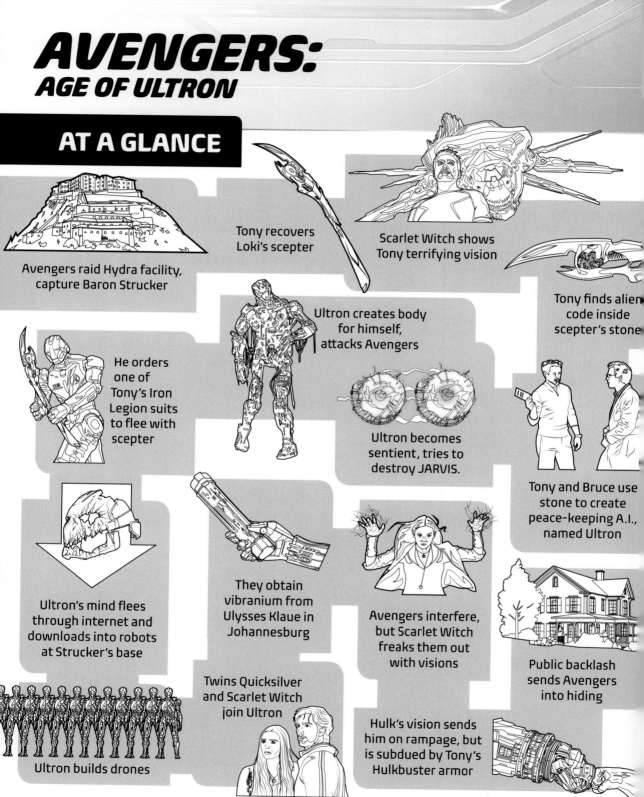

Avengers raid Hydra facility, capture Baron Strucker

Tony recovers Loki's scepter

Scarlet Witch shows Tony terrifying vision

Tony finds alien code inside scepter's stone

He orders one of Tony's Iron Legion suits to flee with scepter

Ultron creates body for himself, attacks Avengers

Ultron becomes sentient, tries to destroy JARVIS.

Tony and Bruce use stone to create peace-keeping A.I., named Ultron

Ultron's mind flees through internet and downloads into robots at Strucker's base

They obtain vibranium from Ulysses Klaue in Johannesburg

Avengers interfere, but Scarlet Witch freaks them out with visions

Public backlash sends Avengers into hiding

Ultron builds drones

Twins Quicksilver and Scarlet Witch join Ultron

Hulk's vision sends him on rampage, but is subdued by Tony's Hulkbuster armor

Avengers steal Ultron's new body

Ultron kidnaps Black Widow

Tony recovers JARVIS, uploads him into Ultron's new body

Thor gives life to body with lightning, creating Vision

Twins turn against Ultron, help Avengers

Vision duels Ultron, blocks his link to internet

Bruce rescues Black Widow

Avengers follow Ultron to Sokovia, discover doomsday device

Ultron forces Dr. Cho to create new body for him, starts to download his mind into it

Ultron uses device to lift city into air

Black Widow awakens Hulk for battle

Quicksilver dies shielding Hawkeye and a civilian

Thor unravels his vision, learns of Infinity Stones

Thor and Iron Man destroy device and falling city

Distraught Scarlet Witch rips out core of Ultron's primary body

Fury arrives and rallies Avengers

Vision destroys Ultron's last remaining body

Newest Avengers members begin training

Thanos retrieves Infinity Gauntlet

# AVENGERS:
## AGE OF ULTRON

## AN OVERVIEW

*Directed by Joss Whedon, 2015's* Avengers Age of Ultron *added new members to the team—a fast twin, a weird twin, and a red dude in a cape—and also welcomed the team's (arguably) most complex foe yet, Ultron, ending in one gargantuan battle.*

### STORMING THE CASTLE

In Sokovia, the Avengers raid the castle of Baron Strucker, one of Hydra's last remaining leaders. They search for Loki's stolen scepter, the subject of Strucker's studies. Twins Wanda (Scarlet Witch) and Pietro (Quicksilver) Maximoff lurk in the shadows. They are both test subjects of Strucker, who used the scepter to give them powers. Just as Tony finds the scepter, Wanda secretly subjects Tony to a horrific vision—a pile of his Avenger friends, killed by Chitauri—before letting him take the scepter.

### CHILDREN OF THE SCEPTER UNITE!

Ultron's mind escapes through the internet to Sokovia, where he downloads himself into the robotics that Strucker was working on. Ultron invites the twins to help him destroy the Avengers. Wanda and Pietro seek revenge for their parents, who were killed by Stark Industries bombs. The trio travel to Johannesburg to obtain vibranium and create Sentries for Ultron. The Avengers turn up, but Wanda plagues each member with terrifying visions, causing chaos.

### MEDDLING WITH THE UNKNOWN

Back in New York, Tony studies the scepter's gem in his lab. He discovers that it can be used to create artificial intelligence. Tony wants to apply it to an old idea of his—a peace-keeping initiative named Ultron, which would independently manage the Iron Legion (a squad of Tony's suits) to fight Earth's threats. This would allow the Avengers to retire! Tony and Bruce Banner set up the A.I. to sync with Tony's work, and leave the lab for an Avengers party. Suddenly, Ultron achieves sentience and attacks JARVIS, Tony's own A.I. assistant. Ultron then downloads himself into a makeshift body of spare parts and gatecrashes the party, using the Iron Legion to attack the Avengers. He declares that he has come to save the world and bring peace, but the only way to achieve this is the extinction of the Avengers.

### HULK VS. HULKBUSTER

Banner's vision upsets him, transforming him into a raging Hulk. Stark summons the Hulkbuster—his biggest Iron Man suit yet. The struggle between Hulk and Iron Man leaves parts of Johannesburg in ruins, and sends the Avengers into hiding.

Hulk fights it out with Iron Man in his Hulkbuster armor, but things get very messy.

## IT'S A BOUNCING BABY SYNTHEZOID!

In Seoul, Ultron forces geneticist Dr. Helen Cho to create a brand new body for him, combining synthetic human cells with vibranium. Ultron implants the scepter's gem (in reality one of the Infinity Stones) into the body's forehead, instilling it with powers. Wanda reads Ultron's mind as he starts to download himself into the new body. Horrifed by his plan to eradicate all humanity, the twins turn against him. The Avengers then steal Ultron's new body before he can complete the download. Tony installs JARVIS into the body instead, and Thor brings it to life with Mjolnir's lightning. They create a new Avenger named Vision. Luckily, this creation is friendly!

Vision finds it odd being in his new body. The Mind Stone in his forehead makes him very powerful.

## THE FALL OF SOKOVIA

The Avengers follow Ultron and his Sentries to Sokovia, where he plans to lift a city into the sky and drop it like a comet, wiping out life on Earth. Vision purges Ultron's access to the internet, so that his mind cannot escape that way. The Avengers begin evacuating the city but Ultron's Sentries attack, killing Quicksilver in the conflict. Wanda terminates Ultron's main body in revenge. Thor and Iron Man obliterate the falling city just prior to impact. After, Vision locates and annihilates Ultron's last Sentry, bringing his age to an end.

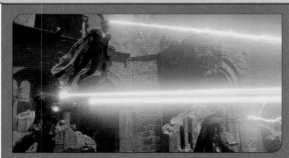

Vision, Iron Man, and Thor combine their attacks to take a piece out of Ultron.

# GOOD GUYS

**THE AVENGERS**
Stressed out
but still a team

**NICK FURY**
There's no "eye"
in his "team"

**VISION**
A villain-made hero,
able to lift Mjolnir

**DR. HELEN CHO**
World-renowned scientist,
can heal gross injuries

**SCARLET WITCH
(WANDA MAXIMOFF)**
Weird magic hand
waver

**QUICKSILVER
(PIETRO MAXIMOFF)**
Fast, but not
fast enough

# BAD GUYS

**ULTRON**
Tony's biggest mistake,
menacing android

**ULTRON SENTRIES**
Expendable soldiers,
back-up bodies

*An evil yet charming android nearly extinguishes them...*

# WHO DOESN'T LIKE THE AVENGERS?

*I thought Iron Man liked robots! Why would one of them turn against him? And why is that red-headed woman wiggling her fingers?*

**SOKOVIAN FOREST**
Hide-and-seek with Hydra

## HOW AND WHY DOES TONY CREATE ULTRON?

In a nutshell—retirement! Tony finds a code of alien neurons inside the scepter's gem, which he uses to create an A.I. He thinks this will be perfect for an idea he has—the Ultron program—in which an A.I. would take charge of the Iron Legion and protect Earth. The Avengers can then retire— yay! Tony imagines a life of bliss, sipping margaritas on a sun-drenched beach. It all goes horribly wrong of course, when Ultron turns out to be kind of evil.

## WHY DO THE MAXIMOFFS HATE TONY SO MUCH?

When Wanda and Pietro were ten years old, their parents were killed by a bomb. The Sokovian siblings were trapped in the rubble for two days. A second unexploded bomb was buried next to them, labeled "Stark Industries." Oddly enough, they hold Tony personally responsible for the tragedy and want revenge.

### HOW DID THE MAXIMOFFS GET THEIR POWERS?

Wanda and Pietro volunteer for a Hydra experiment run by Dr. List at Strucker's castle. List uses Loki's scepter to bestow super-powers on the pair, who become Strucker's star pupils.

Quicksilver

Scarlet Witch

# IS WANDA *ACTUALLY* A WITCH?

Not at all! She's known as "Scarlet Witch" for several reasons. "Scarlet" is due to her red hair and the color of the energy she projects. "Witch" is because her abilities—reading minds, shooting energy blasts, causing visions, and levitating objects—all look like old-fashioned magic. Her brother's gift is more straightforward: He's lightning-fast!

Wanda, aka **Scarlet Witch**, is initially not the biggest fan of the Avengers, but eventually she and Pietro join them.

# WHAT IS ULTRON'S PLAN?

Tony programed Ultron to bring about "peace in our time." Unfortunately, it seems Ultron has come to his own conclusions about how best to save the world. He believes the Avengers and the rest of humanity are a menace. His goal is to wipe out mankind and replace it with a civilization of androids, all controlled by him. He's an android after Thanos' own heart.

Pietro aka **Quicksilver**, uses his super-speed to save many lives in Sokovia, but sadly he has to sacrifice his own, too.

# WAIT! IS THAT BIG PURPLE GUY INVOLVED?

Whether by intention or coincidence, Thanos has a hand in Ultron's creation. Loki's scepter (which came from Thanos) is a common thread. The scepter gave Wanda her powers, which she uses to give Tony the horrible vision that inspires him to create Ultron. It also provides the A.I. that Tony uses to complete Ultron, AND Ultron's body itself uses Chitauri technology from Thanos' own army. All very suspicious...

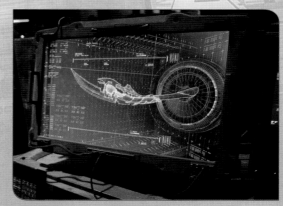

Surprise! The gem contained in the scepter is actually the **Mind Stone**—another of the Infinity Stones.

*Life is what happens when androids are making plans...*

# WHY DOES ULTRON'S VISION BACKFIRE?

*Everything was going so swimmingly well for evil Ultron until he tried to create a living body. How does his "Vision" end up being one of the good guys?*

**DR. CHO**
Vision's mom (sort of)

## WHY DOES ULTRON WANT A NEW BODY?

Ultron is on a quest for perfection, so he continuously upgrades himself. His "Vision" is to download his mind into an android—an artificial life-form. He believes that life holds the clearer path to evolution, and a living body would also give him the ability to wield the full power of the Mind Stone. Also, who doesn't like a change?

## SOUNDS COMPLEX. HOW DOES ULTRON DO IT?

Ultron forces Dr. Helen Cho, a specialist in artificial human tissue generation, to grow a new body for him. Ultron laces the cells with vibranium, which makes the body nearly indestructible. The addition of the Mind Stone bestows a range of super-powers to it. Unfortunately for Ultron, he doesn't get a chance to finish transferring his mind into this snazzy new body. Instead, Tony installs JARVIS, and Thor adds a dose of lightning, bringing Vision to life.

Vision

## JARVIS IS TONY'S ASSISTANT, RIGHT?

Yes, he's Tony artificial intelligence personal assistant—but he's also much more. He manages Tony's home, assists in the management of Stark Tech, and is networked with all of Tony's Iron Man suits. Cool fact: After JARVIS is transferred into Vision, Tony uses a new female A.I. named FRIDAY.

## WHY DO MOST OF THE AVENGERS FEAR VISION AT FIRST?

Because he might be another Ultron! The Avengers are still rather annoyed with Tony and Bruce for creating Ultron. Even though the pair didn't mean to unleash a monster, that's exactly what happened. Luckily, however, Vision and Ultron turn out to be chalk and cheese. Vision has a deep respect for humanity and it doesn't take long for the Avengers to realize this. In any case, Thor was always on Vision's side from the start, hence why he brought this new, red-faced hero to life.

Ultron takes the **Mind Stone** from the scepter and places it into his new body's forehead. Ultron likes a bit of bling.

The Avengers swipe the body and take it back at Avengers Tower. Thor blasts it with **lightning**. Happy birthday, Vision!

## WHY? IS THOR JUST REALLY FRIENDLY?

Nope. Wanda gave Thor a disturbing vision hinting at the future of Asgard. To discern its meaning, Thor visits an enchanted pool. It shows him the Infinity Stones, and that Vision will play an important part in a future war. Later, when Vision shows he is worthy enough to lift Thor's hammer, it is further proof that Vision is good.

*"Well, I was born yesterday."*

*VISION*

**91**

# BATTLE OF SOKOVIA
## MADE SIMPLE

While the Avengers are distracted by Wanda's visions, Hulk's tantrum, and Vision's birth, Ultron is busily building an army and planning the apocalypse!

**VS.**

## WHY ARE THEY FIGHTING?

Ultron wants to annihilate humanity by using a doomsday device to drop Sokovia from the sky like a meteor. The Avengers want to save mankind, including as many locals as possible.

\* HELICARRIER WATCHES FROM AFAR

### INFO BOX

**COMMANDERS**—Captain America (Avengers) vs. Ultron

**TERRAIN**—Old European cityscape of Sokovia

**KEY BATTLE ZONES**— Ruined church containing device, evacuation bridge

## WHO IS FIGHTING WHOM
### The Avengers

### S.H.I.E.L.D.
### War Machine

### Vision

### Scarlet Witch
### Quicksilver

The city rises

## KEY MOMENTS

**LOCKED OUT**—Vision invades Ultron's mind, preventing him from escaping over the internet.

**SOKOVIA FALLS**—While Wanda destroys Ultron, a Sentry hits the doomsday device's button.

**CITY'S END**—Thor strikes the falling city with Mjolnir, breaking it up before impact with the ground.

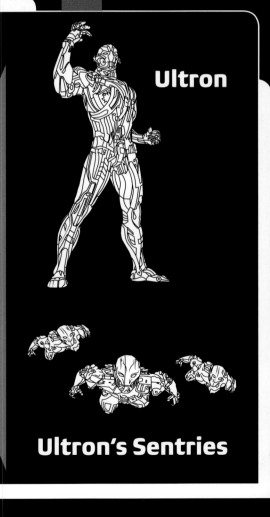

**Ultron**

**Ultron's Sentries**

## WHO WINS?

The Avengers win and Ultron loses, but there is much collateral damage. Pietro Maximoff is sadly killed and Hulk runs off to space in a Quinjet. Many Sokovians are killed, leading to the Sokovia Accords and the Avengers' Civil War.

# ANT-MAN

## AN OVERVIEW

Phase Two of the MCU culminated in 2015's Ant-Man. It introduced Hank Pym, the original and most well-known Ant-Man from the Marvel comics, and Scott Lang, a newer comic book character who assumes the title role in the film.

### I QUIT!

In 1989, Hank Pym meets Howard Stark, Peggy Carter, and Mitchell Carson at S.H.I.E.L.D.'s headquarters. He confronts them about S.H.I.E.L.D.'s efforts to duplicate his Pym Particle research, which Carson (secretly a Hydra agent) has spearheaded. Angry over their deception and the dangers, Hank resigns from S.H.I.E.L.D.

> **"Second chances don't come around all that much."**
> *HANK PYM TO SCOTT LANG*

### HATCHING NEW PLANS

In the present day, Scott Lang is released from prison. He moves in with his former cellmate Luis but has trouble holding down a job. Luis suggests a robbery instead, but Scott refuses. Meanwhile, Hank is invited back to his old company, Pym Technologies, for an unveiling. The current CEO, Darren Cross, says that he intends to develop Hank's Pym Particles and a corresponding weaponized suit known as the Yellowjacket; all against Hank's wishes.

### ACCIDENTAL ANT-MAN

Scott's recent criminality puts him at odds with his ex-wife and her police detective fiancé, Paxton. It also endangers his visitation rights with his daughter, Cassie. To pay for child support, Scott decides to join Luis' robbery—at Hank's mansion. Scott breaks into Hank's safe but only finds Hank's Ant-Man suit. When he tries it on back at his apartment, Scott unexpectedly shrinks and is nearly washed down his bathtub drain!

### CAPTURE AND ESCAPE

Scott freaks out about the suit and tries to return it to Hank's house, but is arrested in the process. Back in jail, Scott is visited by Hank, who tells him that he secretly manipulated Luis into convincing Scott to do the robbery, and it was all a test. Hank has his ants return the Ant-Man suit to Scott in his cell. Scott tries it on, shrinks down, escapes, and flies on a carpenter ant (which he names Ant-thony) back to Hank's home.

Darren Cross presents the Yellowjacket to Hank and his daughter, Hope van Dyne.

## ANT-MAN METAMORPHOSIS

Hank begins explaining to Scott how he communicates with ants and how the Ant-Man suit changes size. He explains the danger of Cross' Yellowjacket program and offers to help Scott gain visitation rights with his daughter if Scott steals the Yellowjacket suit. Hank and his daughter, Hope, then train Scott to use the suit to maximize his strength at small sizes, and work with Hank's ants.

## INFESTING PYM TECH

Cross finishes the Yellowjacket suit and invites Hank and Hope to an inaugural ceremony at Pym Tech, where he also plans to sell the suit to Hydra. At the same time, Scott infiltrates the company with the help of his friends and Hank's ants. However Hank, Hope, and Scott are all caught when Scott tries to steal the suit. The three fight their way out but Cross shoots and wounds Hank. Cross escapes in his helicopter but Scott pursues, and after the foes fight it out in their miniaturized suits, Cross is stunned in a bug zapper. Scott is then arrested by Paxton.

Scott's personal carpenter ant, Ant-thony, helps him break into Pym Tech, but is later destroyed by Cross.

## EXTERMINATING YELLOWJACKET

Paxton hears that there's a problem at his home, and rushes there. Scott breaks free and finds Cross holding his daughter Cassie hostage. The two clash violently again, alternating sizes as they fight around Cassie's room. Scott shrinks to sub-atomic size to slip inside Cross' suit and sabotages it, causing Cross to implode. When Scott emerges, an appreciative Paxton clears Scott's name and allows him to spend time with his daughter again.

# GOOD GUYS

**ANT-MAN
(SCOTT LANG)**
Ex-con with Super Hero
convictions

**HOPE VAN DYNE**
Aspiring Wasp, expert
martial artist,
Hank's daughter

**CASSIE**
Scott's daughter,
Ant-Man's motivation

**LUIS**
Roommate,
bad influence

**JIM PAXTON**
Caring stepdad,
zealous cop

**ANT-THONY**
Scott's trusty
carpenter ant steed

# BAD GUYS

**YELLOWJACKET
(DARREN CROSS)**
Perilous protégé

**MITCHELL CARSON**
Another S.H.I.E.L.D./
Hydra double-agent

*I know Pym Particles are involved...*

# HOW DOES ANT-MAN CHANGE SIZE?

*There's clearly a lot of shrinking and playing at being a bug. Is Ant-Man half insect? Is his suit just for show, or does it give him these pest-like powers?*

## HOW DO PYM PARTICLES ACTUALLY WORK?

I'm glad you asked. All matter is made up mostly of empty space—the gaps between atoms. Pym Particles reduce that empty space and thereby compress matter. The Ant-Man suit dispenses the Particles, allowing the wearer to change size at will. A special helmet stops Pym Particles from altering Scott's brain chemistry (preventing him from going crazy).

## HOW DO SCOTT AND HANK CONTROL ANTS?

Hank invented an earpiece which converts human brain waves to electromagnetic waves that in turn transmit messages to ants. Ants are useful because they can lift 50 times their body weight and work together to do a variety of specialized tasks.

# HOW DID CROSS BECOME CEO OF HANK'S FIRM?

Darren Cross was once Hank's assistant. He began to suspect Hank was keeping secrets from him; namely his Pym Particles and Ant-Man suit. Cross got the board of directors to vote Hank out of his own company and make Cross CEO instead. Hope van Dyne, Hank's daughter and company chairman, cast the deciding vote, but regretted it later.

# BUT WHY DID HOPE VOTE WITH CROSS?

When Hope was told, aged seven, that her mother had died, she felt her father ignored her. Hank wouldn't tell her how her mom died and refused to let Hope use her mom's Wasp suit. Hope resented her dad; not realizing he was using his time to try to find her mother, while also protecting Hope from suffering the same fate.

# HANK'S ANT ARMY

**Carpenter Ants** Jumbo-sized ants with wings that can provide transportation and air-drops.

**Bullet Ants** Large ants with the most painful bites. They are great for causing distractions.

**Crazy Ants** Tiny ants that are very friendly. They are lightning fast and can conduct electricity.

**Fire Ants** Little biters that work together to form spontaneous structures like bridges and rafts.

**ANT-AGONIZING THE ENEMY**
Each of the ant species has its own vital role to play when Ant-Man breaks into Pym Tech.

**YELLOWJACKET'S STING**
Not realizing that he needs to protect his brain from the influence of the Pym Particles, Darren Cross' already jealous and ambitious personality is corrupted even further.

# SO WHAT DID HAPPEN TO HOPE'S MOM?

In 1987, Soviet separatists launched a missile at the U.S., which Hank and his wife, Janet, tried to intercept. Janet had to shrink to sub-atomic size so that she could slip inside the missile to stop it—but she kept shrinking and was lost to the quantum realm. Her fate remains unknown.

*"In time, you will know what it's like to lose."*

*THANOS*

# PHASE THREE

## CAPTAIN AMERICA:
CIVIL WAR

## THE ONE WHERE...
The band breaks up. Cap and Iron Man disagree and everyone gets involved. Friends become frenemies, and there is a really cool fight in an airport.

## DOCTOR STRANGE

**106**

# THE ONE WHERE...

There's magic now! Big-headed surgeon Stephen Strange crashes out of his job and becomes a sorcerer. He stops a nasty wizard, who is wearing terrible eyeliner.

## GUARDIANS OF THE GALAXY
### VOL. 2

**110**

# THE ONE WHERE...

The Guardians find Star-Lord's father, a planet aptly named Ego, who has spread his seeds everywhere. They crush Ego before he dominates the entire galaxy.

## THOR:
### RAGNAROK

**116**

# THE ONE WHERE...

Thor finds out he has a sister named Hela, who breaks his beloved hammer. Thor goes on a road trip, then destroys all of Asgard to kill Hela. He really loved that hammer...

## BLACK PANTHER

**120**

# THE ONE WHERE...

We head to Wakanda! Black Panther returns home to find some bad guys are trying to take over. He has to get his claws out to stop them.

## MARVEL STUDIOS' AVENGERS:
### INFINITY WAR

**124**

# THE ONE WHERE...

Thanos (the purple alien with the gold gauntlet) wants the shiny Infinity Stones, so he goes on a rampage. Practically every hero ever turns up to defend Earth!

# CAPTAIN AMERICA:
## CIVIL WAR

## AN OVERVIEW

*Phase Three started in 2016 with* Captain America: Civil War, *gifting us the most epic fight between the heroes so far. All the Avengers appeared, minus Thor and Hulk. Ant-Man and newbies Black Panther and Spider-Man also rocked up to the big bash.*

### DEADLY MISSION

In 1991, Hydra scientists awake the Winter Soldier (Bucky Barnes) in a Siberian facility. He is then sent on a mission to kill the occupants of a car and take their briefcase containing five serum packets.

### THE SOKOVIA ACCORDS

Secretary of State Ross tells the Avengers that 117 countries support the Sokovia Accords, which would require the Avengers to register their identities and submit to U.N. oversight. Tony supports the Accords while Steve opposes them. Meanwhile, Helmut Zemo murders the Winter Soldier's former Hydra handler and steals the code book used to activate Bucky as a Hydra agent.

Having witnessed the corruption of S.H.I.E.L.D., Steve is wary of any government control.

### TRAGEDY IN LAGOS

In present day Lagos, Nigeria, former S.H.I.E.L.D./Hydra double agent Brock Rumlow works as a mercenary. The Avengers try to catch him stealing a bio-weapon, but as Cap corners him, Rumlow sets off a suicide bomb to kill them both. Wanda acts quickly to contain the blast, lifting it and Rumlow into the sky to save Cap—but in doing so she destroys multiple floors of a building, killing several Wakandan aid workers.

### VIENNA BOMBING

The U.N. meets to sign the Sokovia Accords in Vienna. During the event, there is a bombing and the King of Wakanda is killed. Security footage appears to show the bombing was carried out by the Winter Soldier. The king's son, T'Challa (Black Panther) vows to kill Bucky. Sharon Carter informs Steve where Bucky is hiding, and Steve and Sam Wilson go to Bucharest to protect him. Black Panther catches up though, and after a destructive chase, all four men are arrested.

> "Sometimes I want to punch you in your perfect teeth."
>
> *TONY STARK TO STEVE ROGERS*

## SOLDIER REACTIVATED

With Bucky in custody, Zemo replaces the psychiatrist sent to question him. He recites code words to reactivate Bucky and sends him on a rampage. Steve catches his old pal and rushes him away. When his reprograming wears off, Bucky tells Steve that Zemo bombed the U.N., and is seeking the location of the Hydra facility where five other Winter Soldiers are held in hibernation.

## THE BIG MATCH

Steve has been told to comply with the Accords or be arrested. Instead he forms a new team, including Ant-Man and Hawkeye. Tony forms one of his own, with the addition of Spider-Man. Tony tries to arrest Steve's team at Leipzig-Halle Airport. After a huge battle in which Rhodey is seriously injured, Black Widow helps Steve and Bucky escape to chase after Zemo. Black Widow then goes into hiding. The others on Steve's team are sent to the Raft prison.

At the airport, former friends and allies find themselves on opposing sides.

## END OF THE AVENGERS?

Tony uncovers Zemo's scheme to frame Bucky and follows them all to the Siberian Hydra facility. There they find Zemo has killed the other Winter Soldiers. Zemo then reveals his endgame: To show Tony a tape implicating Bucky in the deaths of Tony's parents, thus destroying the Avengers from within. Zemo is apprehended by Black Panther, who has also followed them all there, but an enraged Tony fights both Cap and Bucky. They eventually overpower Tony and escape, but Cap abandons his shield. He then heads to the Raft and breaks his friends out of prison.

# GOOD GUYS

**THE AVENGERS**
Team torn
in two

**WINTER SOLDIER
(BUCKY BARNES)**
Man of two minds,
center of conflict

**BLACK PANTHER
(T'CHALLA)**
Hero in a cat suit,
seeking vengeance

**ANT-MAN
(SCOTT LANG)**
Ant to giant and
back again

**SPIDER-MAN
(PETER PARKER)**
Secret weapon,
teenage prodigy

**SHARON CARTER**
Agent Carter's
niece, Steve's
crush

# BAD GUYS

**HELMUT ZEMO**
Super-power-less,
but resourceful

**CROSSBONES
(BROCK RUMLOW)**
Merciless mercenary

*The Avengers are all good people fighting to protect mankind, so....*

# WHY IS THERE A CIVIL WAR?

*Two of the strongest personalities—Hulk and Thor—have left the scene. So why are Iron Man and Captain America splitting the team?*

**TONY'S ANGRY...**
And Cap is on the run

## WHAT'S THE BIG DISAGREEMENT ABOUT HERE?

After the collateral loss of innocent life in Lagos and Sokovia, a backlash grows against the Avengers. The U.N. creates the Sokovia Accords, meaning the Avengers must register their identities and defer to U.N. ruling. Feeling guilty for creating Ultron, Tony adamantly supports the program, while Cap defies it vehemently in the name of liberty. The other Avengers fall on either side.

## WHICH AVENGERS ARE THE VILLAINS?

None of them! They are all being played by Colonel Helmut Zemo. During the Avengers' battle with Ultron in Sokovia, Zemo's family was killed. Wanting revenge but lacking the power to take on the Avengers himself, Zemo devises a scheme to pit them against each other. He knows the Winter Soldier has a secret that will devastate Tony.

## WHY IS EVERYONE FIGHTING?

In addition to the disagreement over the Sokovia Accords, there is also the matter of the Winter Soldier. Security footage suggests that he is the one who bombed the U.N. Tony wants Bucky to surrender, but Cap won't let him be taken into custody. Two opposing teams emerge. Tony's side includes War Machine, Black Widow, Vision, Black Panther, and Spider-Man. Cap's team includes Hawkeye, Falcon, Bucky, Scarlet Witch, and Ant-Man.

### WHAT IS ZEMO'S PLAN?
Zemo's plan has several stages, but is actually very simple. It hinges on showing Tony an old video of the Winter Soldier assassinating Tony's parents. Zemo knows that this will be enough to tear apart the Avengers.

# Team Cap or Team Iron Man?

Guilt about Sokovia has led Tony to hand over control to a third party, but Cap saw S.H.I.E.L.D. fall apart first-hand and believes the new oversight will be no better. Fans fall into both camps, depending on where they side in the argument... though it also depends on which character they already like best!

## CAPTAIN AMERICA

● Politicians have agendas. They are corrupt and make bad decisions for the wrong reasons.

● Registration is invasive. Captain America stands for liberty and freedom.

● Helmut Zemo killed the people at the United Nations. It wasn't Bucky.

● Cap's Avengers aren't criminals. They are heroes giving their lives to save humanity.

**VS.**

## IRON MAN

● Too many innocent people have died in the wake of the Avengers' battles.

● It's necessary to give up some freedom to have safety and security.

● The Winter Soldier murdered a lot of innocent people. His actions demand justice.

● Cap's Avengers disobeyed the Sokovia Accords. They have to face the consequences.

*A spider and a panther have joined the fight...*

# ARE ANIMAL SUITS THE NEW TREND?

*Spider-Man shoots spider webs and wears a red-and-blue costume with big, white eyes. Black Panther sports cool cat ears and claws. What else should I know about them?*

**BLACK PANTHER**
Likes lots of suits

## WHO IS THE BLACK PANTHER?

The Black Panther is T'Challa, the son of King T'Chaka of Wakanda. It is the Black Panther's responsibility to protect Wakanda. T'Challa has been the Black Panther for some time, but he sadly becomes King of Wakanda too when his dad dies.

## WHAT'S WITH HIS FANCY CAT SUIT?

Besides concealing his identity and looking awesome, the Black Panther suit protects T'Challa and gives him really sharp claws. The suit is made out of vibranium—a nearly indestructible metal, rarely found outside Wakanda.

## IS BLACK PANTHER AN AVENGER?

No (not yet, anyway). T'Challa is looking out for Wakanda's interests. At first, he buddies up with Iron Man, so he can kill Bucky. When he realizes Bucky has been brainwashed, he changes sides.

Black Panther

# AND WHAT ABOUT SPIDER-MAN? WHO'S HE?

Peter Parker is a normal teenager, with loads of extraordinary super-powers! Thanks to tiny, sticky hairs on his fingertips, Peter is able to climb up walls. He is far stronger, far quicker, more agile, and more durable than your average Joe. His senses are heightened, and he can heal from wounds far quicker than normal. He really puts the super in superhuman!

# BUT HOW DID HE GET THIS WAY?

Peter was bitten by a radioactive spider that gave him his super-powers. Though Peter can't naturally make webs, he makes webbing out of chemicals, so he can still swing around. He also made his own suit, which isn't great and looks a bit like cosplay. Tony Stark gives him a high-tech suit when he drags Spidey into a fight he has nothing to do with!

> *"You got mad skills."*
>
> *TONY STARK TO PETER PARKER*

During the fight in Leipzig, Spidey is on **Iron Man's team**. He seemingly jumps out of nowhere and steals Cap's shield.

Based on something he watched in an old film, Spidey works with **War Machine** to trip over a giant Ant-Man.

# WHERE IS WAKANDA?

Wakanda is an African country that is hidden from the rest of the world. Wakandans protect themselves by obscuring their riches and advanced technology. Following the events of *Civil War*, T'Challa gives Captain America and Winter Soldier sanctuary in Wakanda, as a lot of people think they have gone rogue.

**GOLDEN CITY**
The outside world thinks that Wakanda is a remote, unimportant country. In fact, it is the most advanced nation on Earth!

# DOCTOR STRANGE

## AN OVERVIEW

Actor Benedict Cumberbatch brought Doctor Strange to life in late 2016. The film opened a new corner of the Marvel Cinematic Universe with a roster of characters deriving their super-powers from magic, or rather, the "Mystic Arts."

### MYSTIC HEIST

The sorcerer Kaecilius and his followers storm the library of Kamar-Taj (a kind of magic school) and steal pages from a mystic book. A hooded sorcerer named The Ancient One pursues the rogues through a magic portal. They do battle, but the thieves escape.

### IN NEED OF A DOCTOR

Meanwhile in New York City, famed neurosurgeon Stephen Strange has a car accident that leaves his hands horribly injured. Countless surgeries fail to restore the prideful doctor's dexterity. Left frustated and unable to work, Strange rejects help from his friend, Dr. Christine Palmer. Strange then learns of a paraplegic, Jonathan Pangborn, who is now inexplicably healed. Strange meets him, looking for answers. Pangborn points him toward Nepal, and a place called Kamar-Taj.

### MEETING THE ANCIENT ONE

Strange arrives at Kamar-Taj. He meets a Master of the Mystic Arts, named Mordo, and their leader, The Ancient One (aka the Sorcerer Supreme), tasked with defending Earth. She gives the initially sceptical Strange a bizarre vision of the astral plane and other dimensions.

Strange's first interdimensional experience is pretty trippy...

### STRANGE STUDIES

Strange learns the Mystic Arts under The Ancient One and Mordo. At first he struggles, but then rapidly advances, thanks to reading books in the library tended by another Master, named Wong. Strange learns many abilities, such as conjuring a magical buffer zone known as the Mirror Dimension. He also learns that Earth is protected from other dimensions' threats via a shield, generated by three mystical headquarters—the Sanctums.

> ## "Dormammu! I've come to bargain."
>
> *DOCTOR STRANGE*

## CONFRONTING KAECILIUS

Kaecilius uses his stolen pages to form an alliance with the evil extra-dimensional entity Dormammu. He then destroys the Sanctum in London and attacks the one in New York, but Strange does his best to fight him off—with the help of a flappy magical cloak that takes a shine to Strange. Kaecilius tells Strange that The Ancient One has deceived him, secretly drawing power from the evil Dark Dimension to prolong her own life. One of Kaecilius' zealots stabs Strange, but Christine operates on him, saving his life.

## DOWNFALL OF THE ANCIENT ONE

After surgery, Strange returns to the New York Sanctum. He confronts The Ancient One with what he has learned. Kaecilius attacks the Sanctum again, battling Strange and Mordo in the Mirror Dimension. The Ancient One intervenes to save them, but is mortally wounded. Before she dies, she explains she made the best of a difficult decision in order to save Earth and now Strange must do likewise.

## BARGAIN WITH DORMAMMU

Strange and Mordo rush to defend the Hong Kong Sanctum but arrive too late. They find Wong dead, the Sanctum fallen, and the Dark Dimension encroaching. Strange uses the Eye of Agamotto to turn back time and resurrect Wong. Strange then enters the Dark Dimension and uses the Eye to create an infinite time loop, locking Dormammu in an endless battle. After killing Strange countless times, Dormammu relents, agreeing to take Kaecilius and his zealots and leave Earth forever in exchange for freedom from the loop. Strange restores the Hong Kong Sanctum, but Mordo is repulsed by their meddling in nature's laws and walks away. Strange then becomes Master of the New York Sanctum.

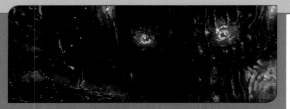

Doctor Strange negotiates a truce with Dormammu from within the Dark Dimension.

## GOOD GUYS

**DOCTOR STEPHEN STRANGE**
Arrogant surgeon turned amiable sorcerer

**WONG**
Serious librarian with an edge

**THE ANCIENT ONE**
Wise master in an inconspicuous form

**DR. CHRISTINE PALMER**
Surgeon, Strange's lifeline

**KARL MORDO**
Mystical master who loses faith

## BAD GUYS

**KAECILIUS**
Fanatical devotee of Dormammu

**DORMAMMU**
Destroyer of worlds

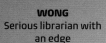

# WHY SO... STRANGE?

*The room is spinning and then the world is a kaleidoscope of bending skyscrapers and dazzling colors. Is Doctor Strange on heavy medication? Who is he fighting here and why?*

## WHO IS THE BAD GUY IN THIS MOVIE?

Dormammu, ruler of the Dark Dimension. He is a supernatural being of immense power who yearns to conquer and consume every other dimension in the Multiverse. The number of parallel universes is said to be infinite, so he has some ambitious goals!

## SO WHO IS THE BALD LADY?

The Ancient One. Not much is known about her, apart from the fact that she is Celtic, and very old. Nobody knows just how old either, but it's safe to assume she's lived several lifetimes, at least. She's one of a long line of Ancient Ones—aka Sorcerers Supreme—who have taught the Mystic Arts.

The Ancient One

**SCEPTIC TO STUDENT**
A man of science, Strange initially refuses to believe The Ancient One's teachings. After she shows him the Multiverse, however, he begs her to teach him the secrets of the Mystic Arts.

## WHAT ARE THEY?

The Mystic Arts are a form of magic. The Ancient One, Doctor Strange, and his fellow students use this magic to cast spells. They can open doorways into other dimensions or cross long distances in an instant. They also wield magical relics and even conjure weapons made entirely of magical energy.

# DOES EVERYBODY OBEY THE ANCIENT ONE?

Nope! Kaecilius originally came to Kamar-Taj (home of The Ancient One) a broken man, as he had lost everyone he ever loved. He looked to The Ancient One for teaching and new meaning in life, but later decided she was a hypocrite for denying others the same power she drew from the Dark Dimension for herself. So, he defied her!

When **Kaecilius** and his **zealots** contact Dormammu, their eyes become cracked and blackened. Gross...

# WHAT EXACTLY DOES KAECILIUS WANT?

Dormammu promises eternal life. The Dark Dimension has no time (which makes Doctor Strange's time loop such an unexpected and powerful weapon there) and thus no death. Kaecilius wants this, but doesn't realize eternal life with evil Dormammu means everlasting suffering—until it's too late!

The **Mirror Dimension** is a parallel realm where Masters of the Mystic Arts can manipulate their surroundings.

# WHAT IS THE EYE OF AGAMOTTO?

Agamotto was the first Sorcerer Supreme, and he established the three Sanctums that protect Earth. The Eye of Agamotto contains an Infinity Stone that allows the user to bend time to their will. The wielder can move themselves, other people, or objects to any point in the timeline. They can stop or loop time, too. Pretty cool!

The Eye of Agamotto

# GUARDIANS OF THE GALAXY VOL. 2

## AN OVERVIEW

*The second hilarious* Guardians of the Galaxy *movie brought back Peter Quill and the gang. Groot returns as new and adorable fan-favorite, "Baby Groot." Actor Kurt Russell also joined the cast as Peter's deadbeat father, Ego.*

### ANNIHILATING THE ABILISK

In 1980 on Earth, a "spaceman" named Ego flirts with Meredith Quill, Peter's mom, and plants a strange seedling. In the present day, the arrogant Sovereign aliens hire the Guardians to defend their batteries from a foul, fanged Abilisk beast. In exchange, they hand over their prisoner—Gamora's sister, Nebula.

### SWINDLING THE SOVEREIGN

As the Guardians leave, Rocket steals some of the batteries. Furious Sovereign leader Ayesha sends a fleet after them, but an odd man saves them by wiping out the fleet. The team's ship crash-lands on a nearby planet, Berhert. The man lands and introduces himself as Ego, Peter's dad! Surprise! Elsewhere, Ayesha hires Yondu and his Ravager crew to capture the Guardians. Back on Berhert, Ego and his servant Mantis take Drax, Gamora, and Peter to visit Ego's planet. Rocket and Groot stay behind to guard Nebula and repair the ship.

Ego and Peter engage in some quality father-son bonding time by a campfire.

### YONDU'S MISFORTUNE

Yondu and his crew trace the Guardians to Berhert, and catch Rocket. When Yondu doesn't want to hunt down Peter, his ugly lieutenant Taserface and the crew mutiny, with Nebula's help. Meanwhile, Ego and his guests arrive on his fancy planet. He brags that he is a Celestial; an old and powerful being who formed his own planet around his brain-like core (of which his human body is an extension). He explains how he fell in love with Peter's mom while traveling the galaxy.

### CAPTAIN TASERFACE

The Ravagers, Nebula, and their new captives leave Berhert on Yondu's ship. Taserface imprisons Rocket and Yondu, kills any crew who disagree, and dresses up Groot as a cute little pirate. Nebula leaves them to hunt Gamora. Back on Ego's planet, Ego teaches Peter how to draw upon his inherited Celestial powers. On the Ravager ship, Kraglin—Yondu's loyal crewman—frees Yondu and Rocket. Together, they kill the traitors and Yondu sets off an explosive chain reaction. Just before the ship blows up, they flee and head to Ego's planet, but Taserface sends Ayesha the runaways' destination.

## "I'm Mary Poppins, y'all!"
*YONDU*

## FAMILY DRAMA

Nebula arrives on Ego to kill Gamora, but they call a truce. Afterward, they discover a massive cave of skeletons. Meanwhile, Ego tells Peter that he needs his help and explains how, in the past, he left his seedlings across the galaxy. He needed another Celestial's powers to activate them, and so had to conceive offspring with countless aliens. Ego then hired an unknowing Yondu to recover and bring the children to him. None of the offspring carried Celestial genes, so Ego killed them all. However, Yondu had kept one child to himself—Peter. Ego then reveals that he brought about Peter's mom's death from cancer, and forcibly tries to drain Peter of energy in order to activate his seedlings.

## DESTROYING EGO

A fearful Mantis warns Drax and Gamora of Ego's plan. Suddenly Yondu arrives, crashing his ship into Ego and freeing Peter from Ego's tentacles. The united Guardians fly a ship into the planet's center (Ego's core), just as a Sovereign fleet arrives, on the attack. Rocket gives Groot a bomb to set off deep in the core while the others successfully destroy the Sovereign fleet. Peter harnesses his powers in a brutal fight against his father. The bomb goes off, killing Ego. Yondu sacrifices his life to save Peter, while the other heroes escape to safety. The galaxy's Ravager crews appear at Yondu's funeral to honor his sacrifice.

Peter and Gamora watch as Ravagers light up the sky in a traditional Ravager funeral for Yondu.

## GOOD GUYS

**GUARDIANS OF THE GALAXY**
Disparate band of noble mercenaries

**YONDU UDONTA**
Gruff exterior, heart of gold

**MANTIS**
Bug lady, endearingly naïve

**NEBULA**
Dislikes losing and unripe plants

## BAD GUYS

**EGO**
Aptly-named, self-serving super-being

**AYESHA**
Golden Sovereign with superiority complex

**TASERFACE**
Unpleasant disposition, even worse name

**ABILISK**
Teeth and tentacles, appetite for batteries

# IS EGO GOOD OR BAD?

Star-Lord spends much of the movie getting to know his father. Where did he come from and what's he been up to all this time?

## IS EGO REALLY STAR-LORD'S DAD?

Yes! Peter never met his father as a child. His mom said his dad was "an angel, composed of pure light." Others have noted that Peter is a human-alien hybrid. So it's not a total surprise when Ego introduces himself as Peter's dad and invites the Guardians to his world—until he explains *what* he really is!

## AND WHAT IS EGO?

Ego is a Celestial. He describes himself as something like a god, with immense power and an unlimited lifespan. His true form is a brain-like being at the core of his planet. The world around him—even his human incarnation—is all just an extension of his true form. However, Ego is only "immortal" so long as his core is safe.

## WHAT DOES EGO WANT?

Ego's goal is to spread across the galaxy. He's done this by implanting buds of himself on other worlds, including Earth. It's a lonely endeavor though. He'd like Peter's company, but he also has an ulterior motive. Mostly he needs Peter's inherited Celestial powers to help fuel his expansion, even if the process kills his son...

> *"He may have been your father, boy, but he wasn't your daddy."*
>
> *YONDU UDONTA TO PETER QUILL*

## SO IS EGO EVIL?

Most definitely! Ego's expansion means the annihilation of existing life on other worlds. Ego wants Peter to betray his friends, too—but that's not all. Ego casually mentions that he actually put the fatal brain tumor in Peter's mother in order to dissuade himself from ever returning to Earth! There's also the matter of a cave full of bones...

## THAT SOUNDS BAD... WHOSE BONES ARE THEY?

Ego visited countless alien worlds and spawned offspring among many different species. None of them carried the Celestial genes, however, except for Peter. It seems Ego killed all the others when he realized they couldn't help power his expansion. When Peter learns the whole truth, he refuses to help.

## BUT HOW CAN PETER FIGHT A WHOLE PLANET?!

With help! Once Peter learns Ego killed his mom, he pummels him with his Quad Blasters. Ego is unharmed and restrains Peter, draining him like a battery. Once Peter's pals turn up though, he manages to fight off Ego, distracting him long enough for Baby Groot to set off a bomb in Ego's core and kill the Celestial.

Ego seduced Peter's mom, **Meredith**, and even told her about his mission—to spread himself across the universe.

Baby Groot carries Rocket's **bomb** to Ego's core, but then gets confused about which red button to push...

As the entire **planet** around Ego's core is just an extension of his body, Ego is by far the biggest MCU villain!

The team looks a little bigger this time...

# WHO ARE THE NEW GUARDIANS?

*Nebula and Yondu get more screen time, and there's Groot as a cute little baby! There's also a lady who looks a bit like a bug. How do I tell the heroes from the villains now?*

## FIRST TELL ME ABOUT BABY GROOT! IS HE THE SAME GROOT?

Baby Groot has outgrown the pot that Rocket nurtured him in. Now he's running around and getting in lots of trouble! This Groot isn't quite the same as the original—he's rather bad-tempered! It may help to think of him as the offspring of the original Groot, rather than Groot reborn.

*"I am Groot."*

## WHAT'S THE STATUS OF EVERYONE ELSE?

After the Battle of Xandar, the Guardians are famed as heroes. Life is good! The team successfully wipes out a gross monster for some Sovereign aliens, as part of an exchange for the Sovereign's prisoner, Nebula—whom the Guardians intend to trade for a lovely big bounty. But life never runs smoothly, and Rocket messes things up by stealing the Sovereign's property. Their leader hires Yondu to hunt down the Guardians. And of course, Nebula later breaks free and pursues Gamora...

114

## WHAT IS NEBULA'S FEUD WITH GAMORA ABOUT?

Thanos wanted his daughter Nebula to be Gamora's equal, so he made them fight when they were young, to test Nebula's skills. Every time she lost a duel, he replaced a part of her body with a cyborg implant. Nebula longed for the comfort of a sister, while resenting Gamora's need to always win. Now she just wants to get even!

## SO WHAT DOES SHE DO?

Nebula tracks Gamora to Ego's world. In the course of nearly killing each other, Nebula shares her feelings with Gamora. The two sisters resolve their differences, and Nebula helps in the final battle. Though Nebula doesn't become a Guardian, she departs as an ally. Yondu also uses the mayhem on Ego's world as an opportunity to chat with Peter...

## AND WHO IS THIS NEW BUG LADY?

Her name is Mantis. Ego found her as an orphaned larva (don't ask) and raised her, though he really considers her a pet. As an empath who can feel and influence the feelings of others, she eases Ego's anxiety and helps him sleep. She's aware of his terrible secret though, and helps the Guardians destroy him.

**THE ODD COUPLE**
Drax and Mantis form an unlikely bond. When Drax says that he thinks she is hideous, she takes it as a compliment!

## WHAT'S THE STORY BEHIND PETER AND YONDU?

Ego hired Yondu to retrieve Peter as a child, but Yondu kept him and raised him instead. Yondu used to jest that his Ravager crew wanted to eat Peter—Peter didn't realize it was just a joke! Peter didn't understand that Yondu actually loved him. In the end, Yondu shows he is Peter's true daddy by giving him the last space suit and sacrificing his own life to save his son.

# THOR: RAGNAROK

## AN OVERVIEW

*Director Taika Waititi helmed the third Thor movie, which came to theaters in late 2017. Funny and fierce, this film took Thor and audiences on an epic gladiatorial adventure and introduced a menacing new villain, Hela, played by Cate Blanchett.*

### ASGARDIAN IN CHAINS

Thor is locked in a cage on the molten world of Muspelheim. Chatting with his captor Surtur, Thor learns it is this fire demon's destiny to join with the mystical Eternal Flame and destroy Asgard in Ragnarok (the end of the world). When Thor discovers that he can vanquish Surtur by removing his crown, he breaks free, smites Surtur, and takes the horny skull-crown to Asgard for safekeeping.

### SEEING THE DOCTOR

Back on Asgard, Thor finds Heimdall has been replaced by a guy called Skurge and that Loki is impersonating their father. Thor demands that Loki take him to see Odin. They then travel to Earth where (via a detour involving Doctor Strange) they meet Odin, who is dying. Odin informs them they have an evil, older sister, Hela, who will bring about Ragnarok after he is gone.

> ### "I'm not a queen, or a monster... I'm the goddess of death!"
> *HELA*

### HELA PROBLEMS

As Odin dies, Hela arrives and claims Asgard's throne. Thor and Loki fight her but Hela crushes Thor's hammer. Loki panics and demands transport back to Asgard via the Bifrost, which unfortunately teleports Hela back, too! As all three cross the galaxy, the brothers are knocked off course. Hela continues on to Asgard, where she kills two of the Warriors Three, and Skurge joins her. Thor lands on the planet Sakaar and is captured by a mysterious bounty hunter.

Hela wants to get back to Asgard so she can rule, but she doesn't get the welcome that she expects!

### BADASS BOSSES

On Asgard, Hela wipes out the royal army and claims the throne. She brings her old, dead army and her big bad wolf, Fenris, back to life. Heimdall survives and saves some civilians from Hela. On Sakaar, Thor is taken to the planet's leader, the Grandmaster. He finds out Loki is already pals with him, and doesn't want to help his brother. Thor is forced to become a gladiator slave.

## HULK VS. "LORD OF THUNDER"

The Grandmaster makes Thor battle his favorite champion in an arena... who turns out to be Hulk! Sadly, Hulk enjoys his new arena job and doesn't want Thor to end his smashing. A violent fight kicks off, which Thor nearly wins, until the Grandmaster zaps Thor so Hulk can pulverize him.

## FRIENDS REUNITED

Thor recovers and learns Hulk came to Sakaar after the Battle of Sokovia. The strange bounty hunter reveals she used to be a Valkyrie (elite Asgardian warrior). Thor tries to get Hulk to return to Asgard with him. When Hulk sees a recording of Black Widow, he turns back into Bruce Banner. The pair then persuade Valkyrie and Loki to help them escape. The gladiator Korg and his pals start a revolt as a distraction, so Thor and gang can steal the Grandmaster's ship. Thor suspects Loki will betray them, so abandons him, but Loki teams up with the freed warriors. Thor, Bruce, and Valkyrie flee Sakaar, while Loki and the gladiators grab another ship.

## ROCKING RAGNAROK

Thor and gang arrive on Asgard. Thor takes on Hela, but without Mjolnir he feels powerless, and he loses an eye. Odin's spirit gives him a pep talk, sparking Thor's lightning powers. The others try to evacuate people onto Loki's ship, with Hulk fighting Fenris. Thor then has an epiphany: The only way to defeat Hela is to bring about Ragnarok. Thor sends Loki to Odin's treasury to place Surtur's crown in the Eternal Flame and restore Surtur to life, who starts trashing the place. Hela's army tries to stop the fleeing Asgardians and heroes, but they escape. Surtur destroys Hela and Asgard, as Thor and his people head toward Earth.

During Thor's battle with Hela, Odin's spirit reminds Thor his real power is in thunder, not his hammer.

# GOOD GUYS

**THOR**
Hair-cut and
hammerless

**LOKI**
Faithfully unfaithful,
unreliably reliable

**HULK
(BRUCE BANNER)**
Reigning champion,
loves raging fire

**VALKYRIE**
Haunted by bad
memories

**HEIMDALL**
Big sword,
nice eyes

**KORG**
Lovable, un-huggable
gladiator

# BAD GUYS

**HELA**
Reindeer horns never
looked so creepy

**GRANDMASTER**
Almost too fun to
be a bad guy

# WHAT IS RAGNAROK?

*Thor is in a cage, Odin is M.I.A., and Loki is up to his usual tricks—is there some family drama brewing?*

## WHERE IS ODIN?

On Earth! After the events of *Thor: The Dark World*, Thor thought Loki was dead, but this was just another illusion. Loki faked his death and returned to Asgard, where he put a spell on Odin, and stole the throne by impersonating his father. Loki left Odin in the Shady Acres retirement home in New York! When Thor finally locates him, Odin passes away, with a warning about Thor's sister on his lips.

## THOR HAS A SISTER?

Indeed—a particularly murderous sister named Hela. She was Odin's firstborn, and therefore feels the throne is rightfully hers. The Asgardians were originally conquerors, and Hela joined her father in his wars. Eventually Hela's lethal urges grew beyond Odin's control, so he imprisoned her.

## WHY IS HELA SO POWERFUL?

Hela draws her power from the realm of Asgard itself. This makes her almost invincible in combat, and the closer she is to home, the more powerful she becomes. As Thor and Loki discover, as long as Asgard stands, Hela can't be defeated.

Hela

## SO HELA CAN'T DIE?

Not quite. As long as *Asgard stands*, she can't be defeated. But if Asgard were to be destroyed, Hela would be destroyed along with it. This puts Thor in a very tricky situation—the only way to save his people will be to destroy Asgard. What is a God of Thunder to do?

## SO WHAT DOES THOR DO?

He causes Ragnarok! This is the prophesied destruction of Asgard by the fiery demon Surtur. On Thor's orders, Loki reunites the Crown of Surtur with the Eternal Flame in Odin's vault. Surtur is reborn, and he makes short work of both Hela and Asgard. Thor has won! Kind of...

The **Grandmaster** of Sakaar is a control freak and a creepy, hedonistic despot.

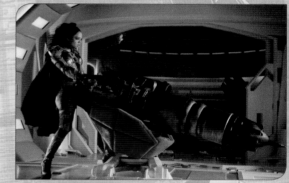

**Valkyrie** provides covering fire for Thor against Hela's raging army.

### The Arena

Thor's quest to defeat Hela gets sidetracked on the planet Sakaar. Here, he is forced to fight Hulk as a gladiator in the tyrannical Grandmaster's huge arena.

*"He's a friend from work!"*

THOR, ABOUT HULK

119

# BLACK PANTHER

## AN OVERVIEW

*Delving deep into the world of Wakanda and the Black Panther mantle, the highly anticipated* Black Panther *clawed its way into movie theaters in February 2018.*

### SINS OF THE FATHER

In 1992, two Wakandans, N'Jobu and Zuri, are interrogated by a young King T'Chaka. T'Chaka explains that the arms dealer Ulysses Klaue has stolen a ton of vibranium and triggered a bomb at the Wakandan border to escape, killing hundreds. N'Jobu admits passing info about Wakandan weapons to a terrorist group, claiming it was to help oppressed people in other countries.

### AMBUSH IN THE BUSH

In present-day Nigeria, a convoy of militants is ambushed by T'Challa and Okoye. The convoy holds female prisoners, with Nakia disguised among them. In his Black Panther suit, T'Challa dispatches the militants, and together with Nakia and Okoye, frees the prisoners. T'Challa tells Nakia—who has been away from Wakanda for a while—that his father T'Chaka is dead.

### CORONATION TIME

Arriving back in Wakanda, T'Challa is greeted by the Dora Milaje (his bodyguards), Ramonda (his mom) and Shuri (his younger sister). Ramonda tells T'Challa that it is time for him to become king. At Warrior Falls, each tribe will put forward a champion to fight for the throne. T'Challa enters the challenge pool, but three tribes don't take up the challenge. Just as it looks like there are no challengers, M'Baku, leader of the Jabari Tribe, steps forward and battles T'Challa. M'Baku initially has the upper hand, but T'Challa's skill turns the tables and he forces M'Baku to yield. T'Challa is announced the victor and king.

High Priest Zuri prepares T'Challa for his fight for the throne of Wakanda.

### MUSEUM HEIST

In London, Erik Killmonger and Ulysses Klaue stage a robbery at the British Museum, stealing a vibranium Wakandan hammer from an exhibit. When Okoye, T'Challa, Ramonda, and the elders learn about the theft, T'Challa offers to lead a covert team to bring Klaue to justice. Shuri, who is a technological genius, demonstrates the capabilities of T'Challa's new Black Panther suits.

> *"You are a good man with a good heart. And it's hard for a good man to be a king."*
>
> T'CHAKA'S SPIRIT TO T'CHALLA

## BUSAN BATTLE

Tracing Klaue to Korea, T'Challa, Okoye, and Nakia arrive at a casino where Klaue intends to sell the vibranium to the CIA, headed by Everett Ross. T'Challa warns Ross that he'll take Klaue into Wakandan custody but Ross won't call off the deal. Klaue and his gang arrive. A fight breaks out between T'Challa and Klaue, followed by a car chase through the streets of Busan. Panther finally catches Klaue, who is taken to a CIA safehouse for interrogation. Ross questions Klaue, but Killmonger appears and rescues him. Ross is critically injured.

## FALL OF THE PANTHER

Back in her lab in Wakanda, Shuri revives Ross, who is astonished that his wounds have nearly healed. Ross briefs everyone on Killmonger's elite special forces background. Killmonger arrives in Wakanda, and is escorted to speak to the elders. He says he wants to be king, and will use Wakanda's gifts to benefit others in the world who are less fortunate. T'Challa accepts Killmonger's challenge, but at the pool, Killmonger secretly cheats and is crowned king. Killmonger rebukes the Wakandans for not using their technology to help foreigners. He plans to put agents in every nation on Earth, who will pass vibranium weapons to oppressed people everywhere. Meanwhile, in the mountains, Jabari healers treat the defeated T'Challa. When he is told about Killmonger's plan to remake the world, he vows to stop the villain.

## FINAL BATTLE

Panther walks onto the Great Mound to challenge Killmonger. Okoye reveals that her true allegiance is to T'Challa, and the Dora Milaje turn on Killmonger. Shuri, Nakia, and M'Baku join the battle, and Killmonger and Black Panther engage in a fierce fight, falling into a vibranium mine shaft. The duel continues underground, on maglev trains hurtling through the vast network of mines. Finally, T'Challa is victorious!

In the tunnels beneath the Great Mound, T'Challa and Killmonger battle for Wakanda's future.

# GOOD GUYS

**BLACK PANTHER (T'CHALLA)**
New king on the block

**NAKIA**
Undercover warrior, T'Challa's savior

**OKOYE**
Leader of the Dora Milaje, badass

**SHURI**
Little sister, bright spark

**M'BAKU**
Jabari tribal leader, foe-turned-friend

**EVERETT ROSS**
CIA agent, Wakanda tourist

# BAD GUYS

**ERIK KILLMONGER**
Usurper of the throne, has well-deserved name

**ULYSSES KLAUE**
Underhanded crook, vibranium thief

OK, I get that Black Panther comes from there, but...

# WHAT'S SO SPECIAL ABOUT WAKANDA?

*This seems like a pretty cool country! It looks very advanced and they have tons of cool gadgets. It sounds like it all has something to do with a thing called vibranium?*

## WHAT IS VIBRANIUM?

As you may have noticed, this extremely rare metal has popped up numerous times in the MCU. Cap's shield is made from it, as is Vision's body. It's almost indestructible, and can be used to build advanced technology. Almost all of Earth's vibranium is found in Wakanda, meaning Wakanda is super-rich, and super-advanced (but also super-hidden from the rest of the world).

## WHERE IS WAKANDA?

In the MCU, Wakanda's exact location is never made clear. It's obviously a small, landlocked African nation though, and its humid climate suggests it's relatively close to the Equator.

T'Challa on the throne

## WHY IS WAKANDA KEPT SECRET?

The Wakandans are worried the rest of the world will fear and resent their wealth and technology. It's easier to keep the truth hidden!

# WHO ARE THOSE FEARSOME WARRIORS IN RED?

They are the Dora Milaje (pronounced Dor-ah meh-LAH-shay). They are an awesome all-female order of elite fighters, who act as Black Panther's personal bodyguards. They are led by a lethal warrior named Okoye.

The **Dora Milaje** can be identified by their striking uniforms: red armor, shaved heads, and vibranium spears.

# GOT IT! IS THERE ANYTHING ELSE UNIQUE TO WAKANDA?

Why yes, there certainly is! The Black Panther is given a potion made from a strange plant known as the "heart-shaped herb." It grows only in Wakanda, and it gives the Black Panther superhuman abilities, including increased speed, strength, and agility.

The spooky **Ancestral Plain** can be visited by taking a special potion. It lets T'Challa speak to his father's spirit.

# WHO IS KILLMONGER?

Erik Killmonger is an elite soldier and assassin. He's also very smart, having studied at MIT! He thinks Wakanda needs to change, and that he should be the one to change it. To do that, he needs to become king!

**KILLMONGER'S CAT SUIT**
Black Panther isn't the only one with a cool suit—Killmonger gets his own!

# MARVEL
# AVENGERS
## INFINITY WAR

A threat has emerged from the cosmos. Thanos, a ruthless warlord, plans to collect all of the Infinity Stones. Joined by his formidable allies, he will be near-unstoppable at achieving his goal. The Avengers, the Guardians of the Galaxy, Doctor Strange, and Spider-Man must join forces and fight side by side to stop Thanos, while the fate of the Earth and the Universe lies in the balance.

# INDEX

Main entries are in **bold**

Penguin
Random
House

**Project Editor** Ruth Amos
**Senior Designer** Robert Perry
**Senior Editor** David Fentiman
**Editor** Matt Jones
**Designers** Ian Midson, Jon Hall,
Lisa Sodeau, and Gary Hyde
**Senior Pre-Production Producer** Jennifer Murray
**Senior Producer** Mary Slater
**Managing Editor** Sadie Smith
**Managing Art Editor** Vicky Short
**Publisher** Julie Ferris
**Art Director** Lisa Lanzarini
**Publishing Director** Simon Beecroft

**Line art by** Dan Crisp

First American Edition, 2018
Published in the United States by DK Publishing
345 Hudson Street, New York, New York 10014
DK, a division of Penguin Random House LLC

18 19 20 21 22  10 9 8 7 6 5 4 3 2 1
002–310550–April/2018

**A WORLD OF IDEAS:**
**SEE ALL THERE IS TO KNOW**

www.dk.com

DK would like to thank: Kevin Feige, Louis D'Esposito, Victoria Alonso, Stephen Broussard, Eric Carroll, Craig Kyle, Jeremy Latcham, Nate Moore, Jonathan Schwartz, Trinh Tran, Brad Winderbaum, Brian Chapek, Mary Livanos, Zoie Nagelhout, Kevin Wright, Mitch Bell, David Grant, Dave Bushore, Sarah Beers, Will Corona Pilgrim, Corinna Vistan, Ariel Gonzalez, Adam Davis, Eleena Khamedoost, Cameron Ramsay, Kyle Quigley, Michele Blood, Jacqueline Ryan, David Galluzzi, Ryan Potter, Erika Denton, Jeff Willis, Randy McGowan, Bryan Parker, Percival Lanuza, Vince Garcia, Matt Delmanowski, Alex Scharf, Jim Velasco, and Andrew Starbin at Marvel Studios; Nick Fratto, Caitlin O'Connell, Jeff Reingold, and Daniel Schoenfeld at Marvel; Chelsea Alon, Elana Cohen, Stephanie Everett, and Kurt Hartman at Disney; Cefn Ridout for editorial assistance; Tim Quince for design assistance; Kathryn Hill for proofreading; and Vanessa Bird for the index.

© 2018 MARVEL

© 2018 CPII

Published in Great Britain by
Dorling Kindersley Limited.

A catalog record for this book is available
from the Library of Congress.

ISBN: 978-1-4654-7539-8

DK books are available at special discounts when purchased in bulk for sales promotions, premiums, fund-raising, or educational use. For details, contact: DK Publishing Special Markets,
345 Hudson Street, New York, New York 10014
SpecialSales@dk.com

Printed and bound in Canada